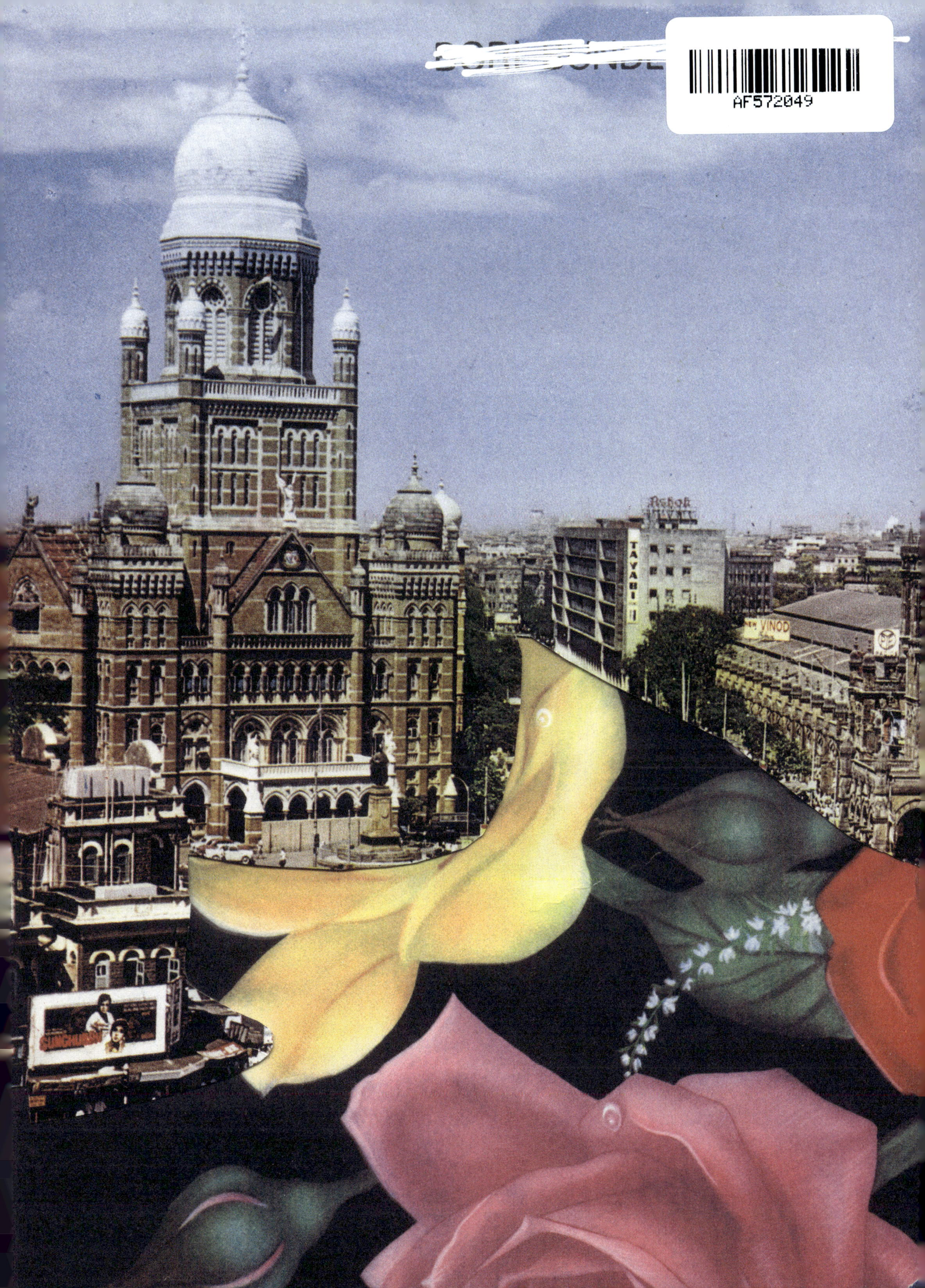
TAYABI
VINOD

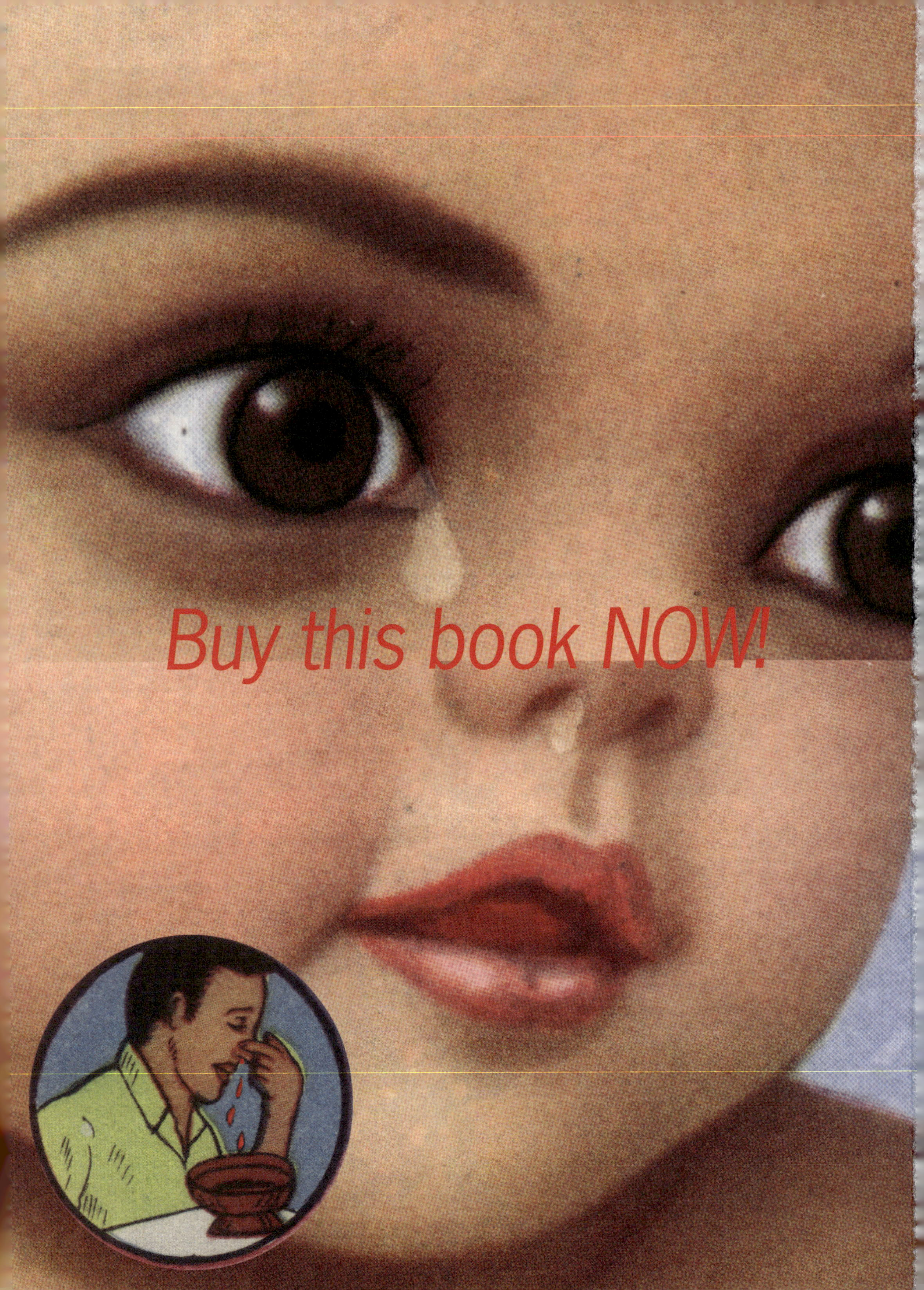
Buy this book NOW!

I LOVE MY INDIA

stories for a city

Avinash Veeraraghavan

TARA PUBLISHING / DEWI LEWIS PUBLISHING

CUT ALONG DOTTED LINE

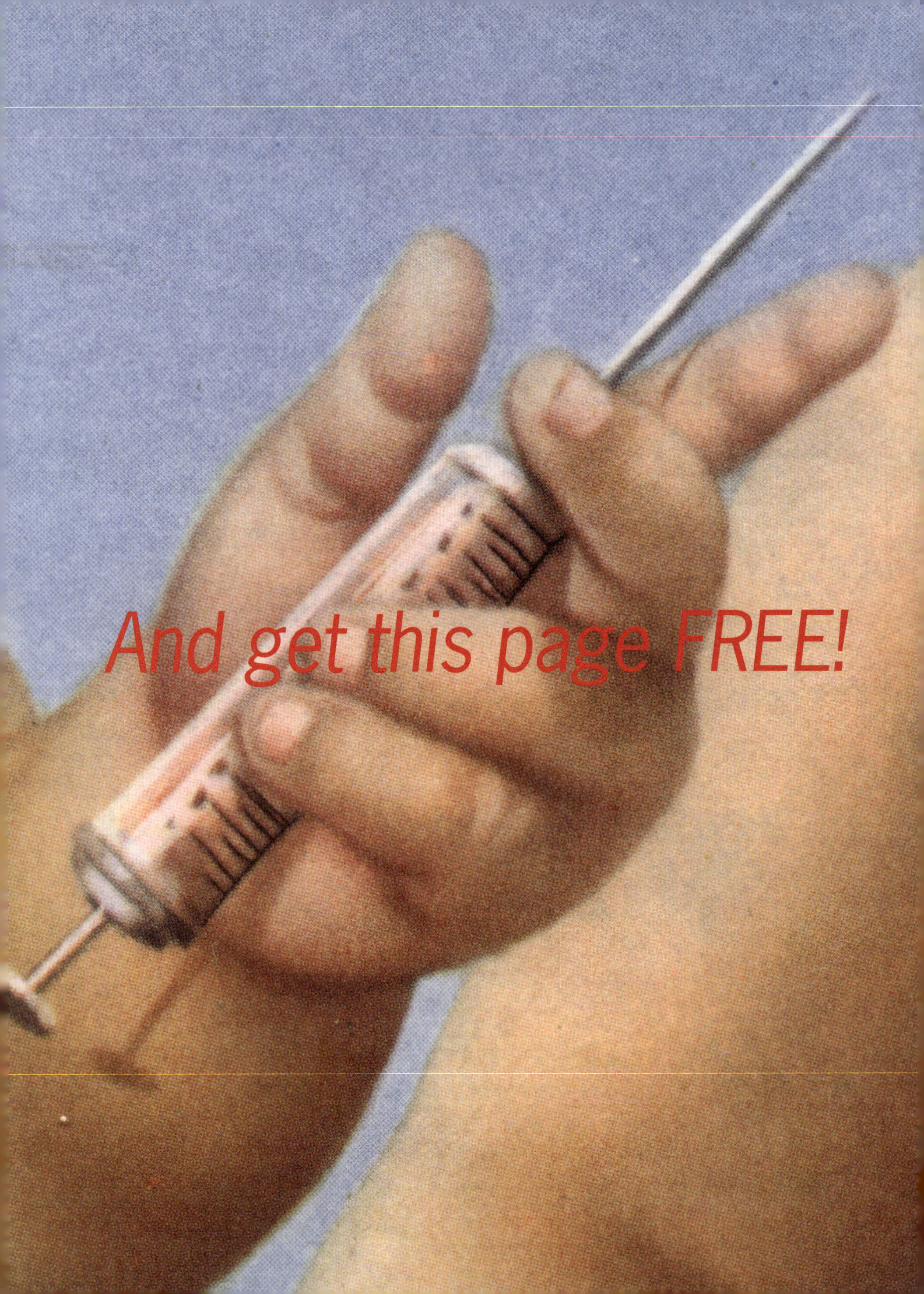
And get this page FREE!

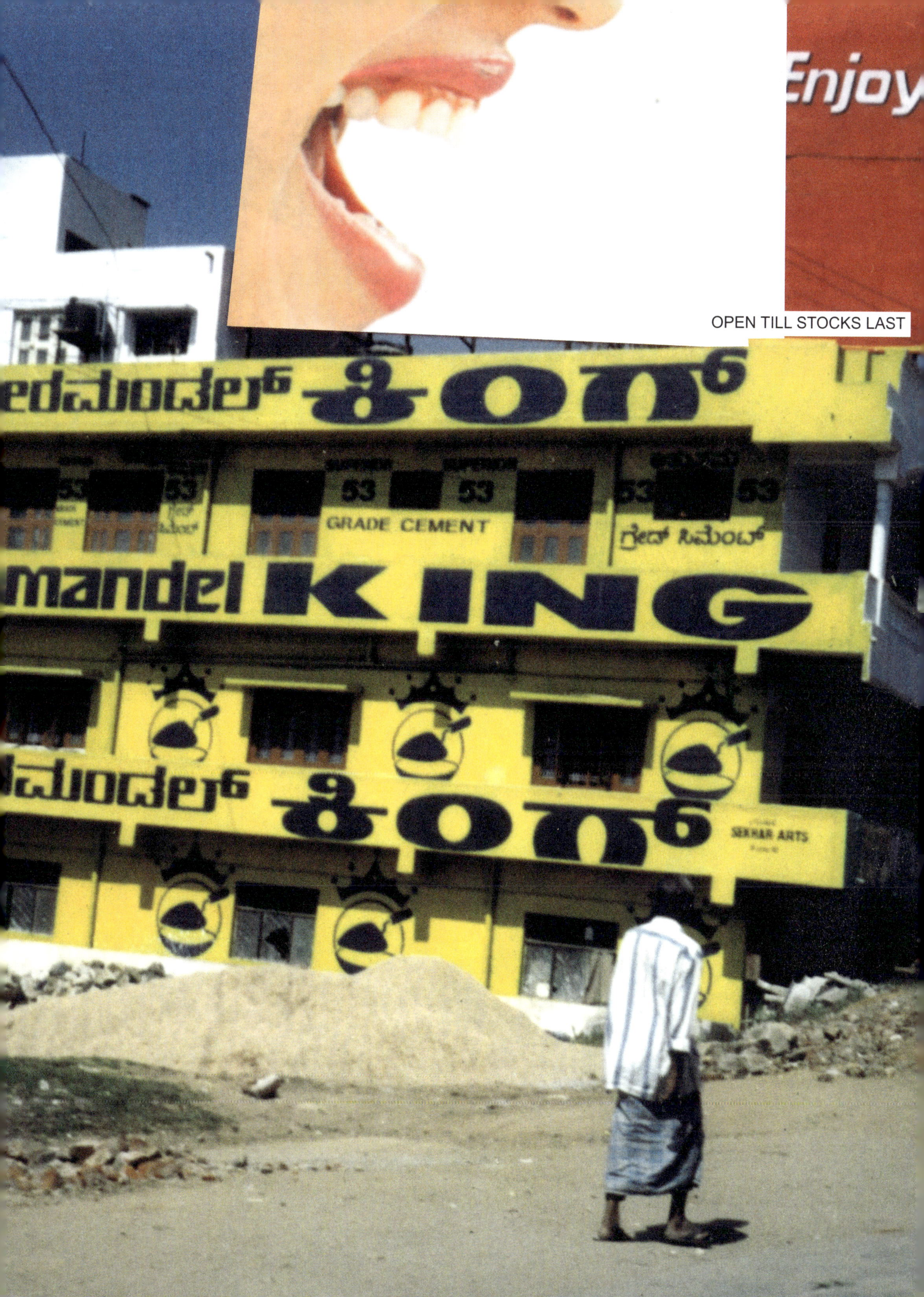
Enjoy
OPEN TILL STOCKS LAST
ಕಿಂಗ್
53
GRADE CEMENT
ಗ್ರೇಡ್ ಸಿಮೆಂಟ್
mandel KING
ಕಿಂಗ್
SEKHAR ARTS

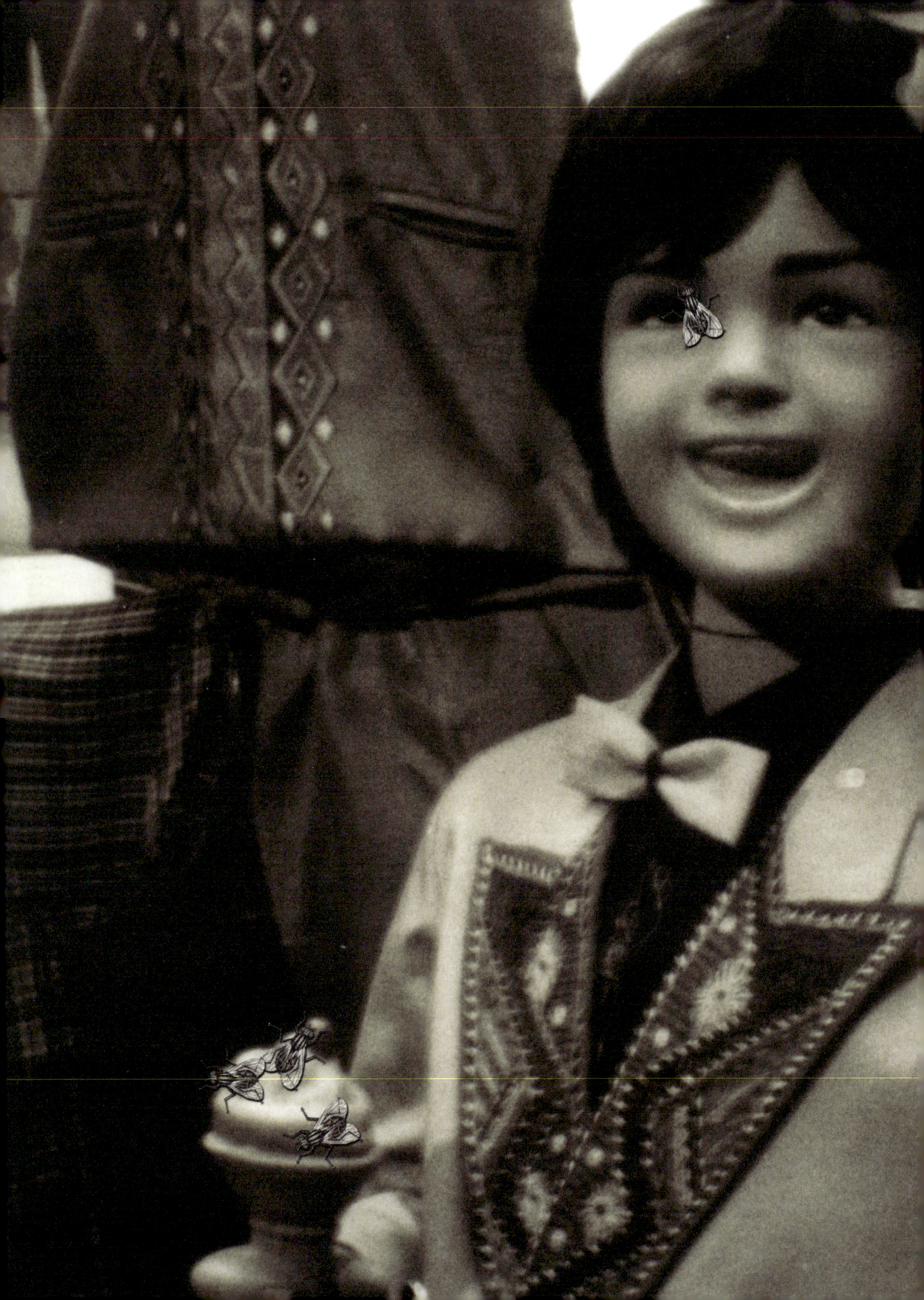

Contents

Introduction

Trapped in the all visible reality of media, in a time of compulsive voyeurism, where geography is nothing more than matter to be sold by tour-operators, and where the urge of knowing is often, if not always, replaced by that of purchasing, we are taken by a young story-teller for a walk around the places he lives in. It is a simple act that can turn out to be of great revelatory impact.

Equipped with the curiosity of an explorer, the author engages in a romance with his own habitat, neither to document buildings and streets, nor to just gather postcards of his town. Throughout this book we experience the flavour of stories that once resided in an unsaid realm, under the subtle layer of tangible reality and that are now brought up to the surface by the simple but powerful modus of 'cut and paste'. Pictures are juxtaposed without any hierarchy. Portraits, still lives, movie star posters as big as palace facades, advertising billboards, buildings and trees are lined out to generate an acid and poetic vision, where the inside and the outside, the man-made and the natural are not perceived as divided.

The atmosphere we are pulled into may recall the world of surrealist artists whose aim was to liberate the unconscious erotic energy from the strait-jacket of societal norms and rules, but here we sense something more—an open work that wishes to extend the potential of forms beyond its own limitations. Although the author is aware of the surrealistic nature of his work, he refuses to impose any theoretical strategy upon himself. He plunges into a play of revealing and yet concealing, of showing and yet letting the narrative remain hidden for further explorers. We come across neither a fixed meaning, nor a given interpretation of visual signs, but rather a whispering of unending possibilities.

Even the organisation of the book into three parts does not lead to a logical closing of intent. It is more a question of rhythm, of musical rhythm. In a realm of Calvino-esque echoes, the 'invisible cities' begin to unravel their presence, at times stripping away their clothes, at times dressing up, until the entire space is filled with accessories of powerful and resounding languages.

And of languages, we end up talking, not of visual realms, but of languages as viruses (William Burrough's genius intuition) affecting the texture of matter, reverberating in musical forms. It is by pronouncing the word music that this book suddenly reveals its own secret nature: it is an extended version of a rap. Triggered by the interaction between urban Indian pop culture and the one generated by ever-growing cyberspace, the sensitivity of a young visionary begins to speak out, articulating his own tongue in a seductive idiom. If language is a virus, then the stream of pictures we are going to read-see-speak in this book is equally contagious: I find it already affecting the way I look out at the street.

Andrea Anastasio
Rome

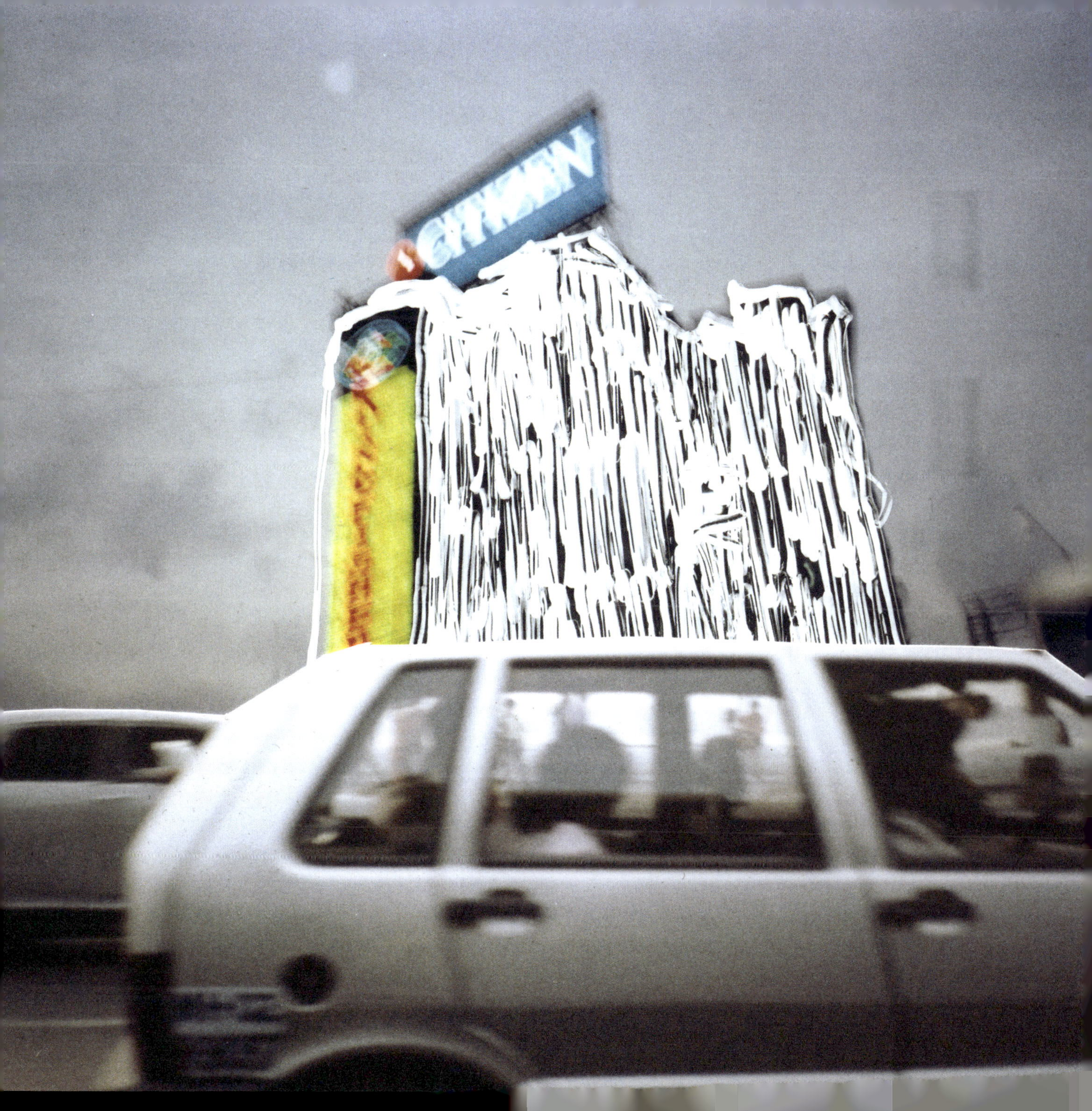

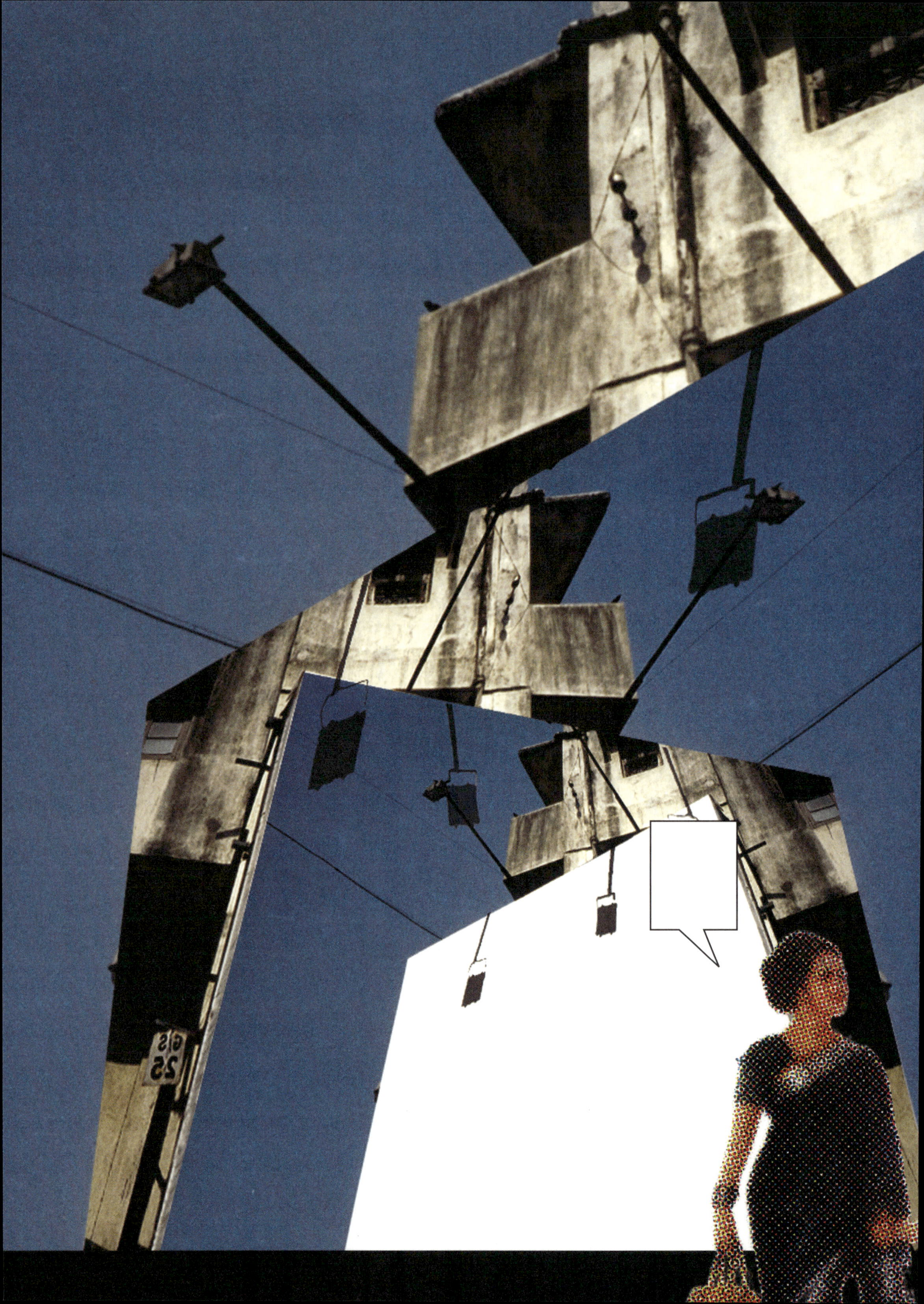

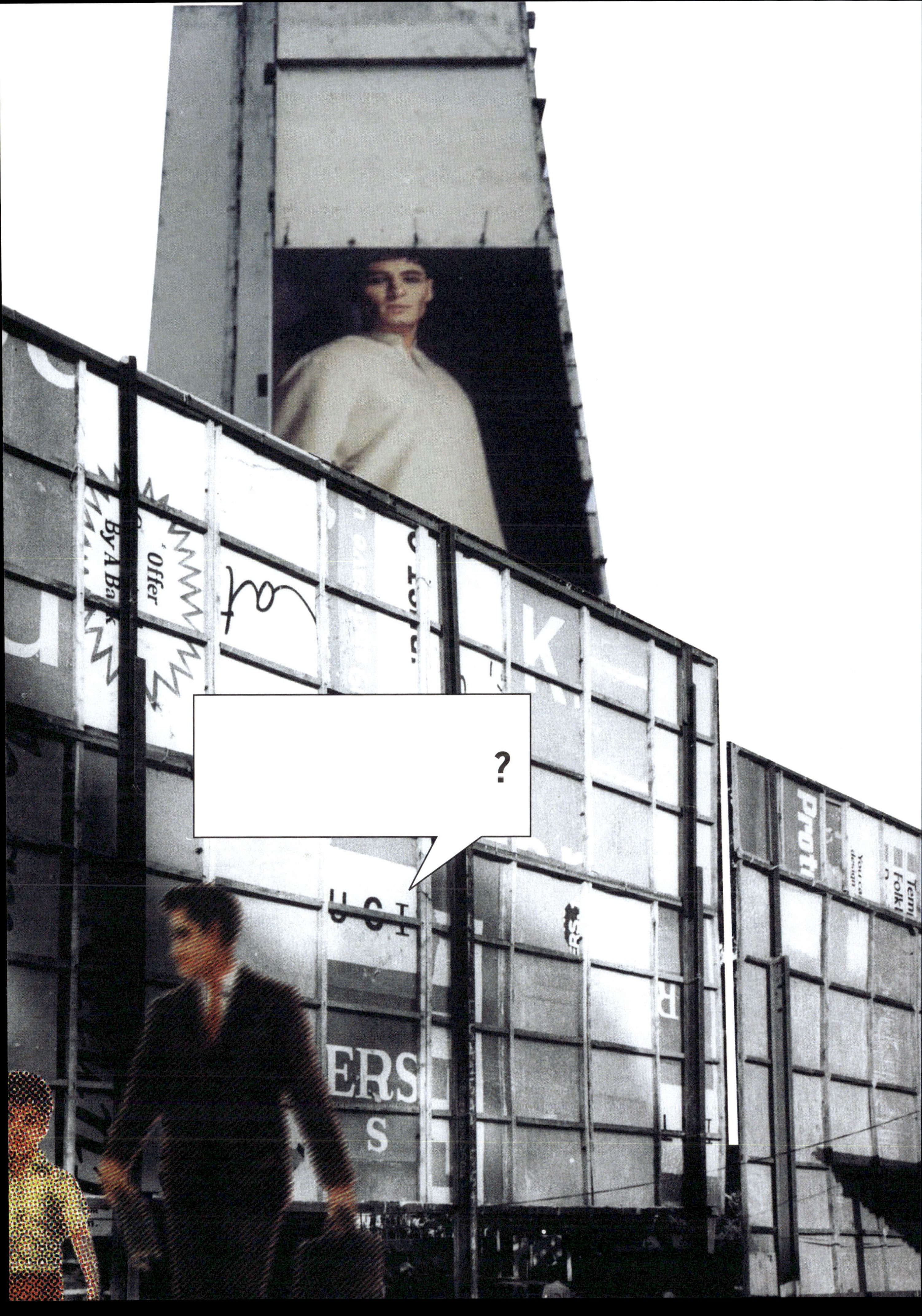
?
Offer

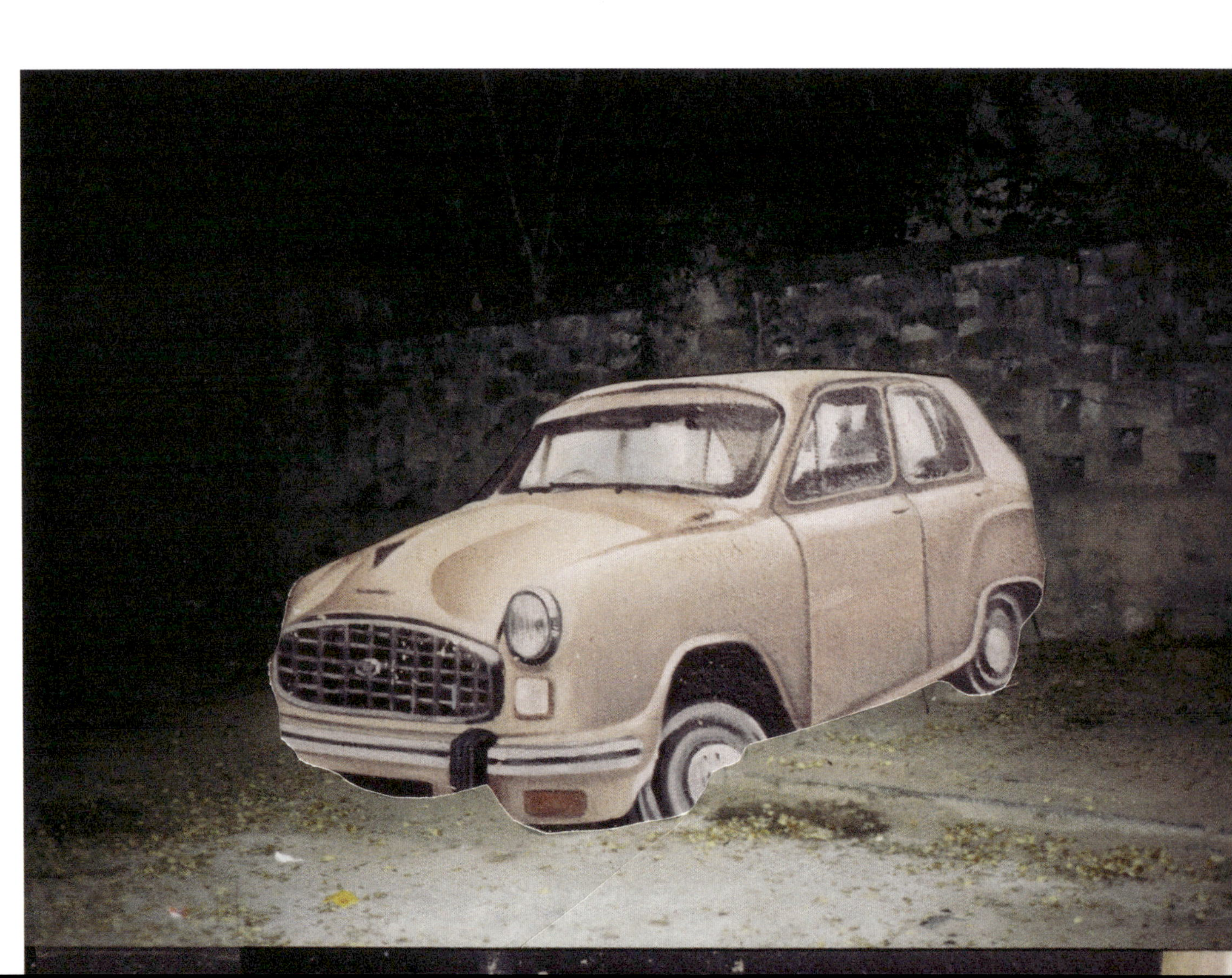

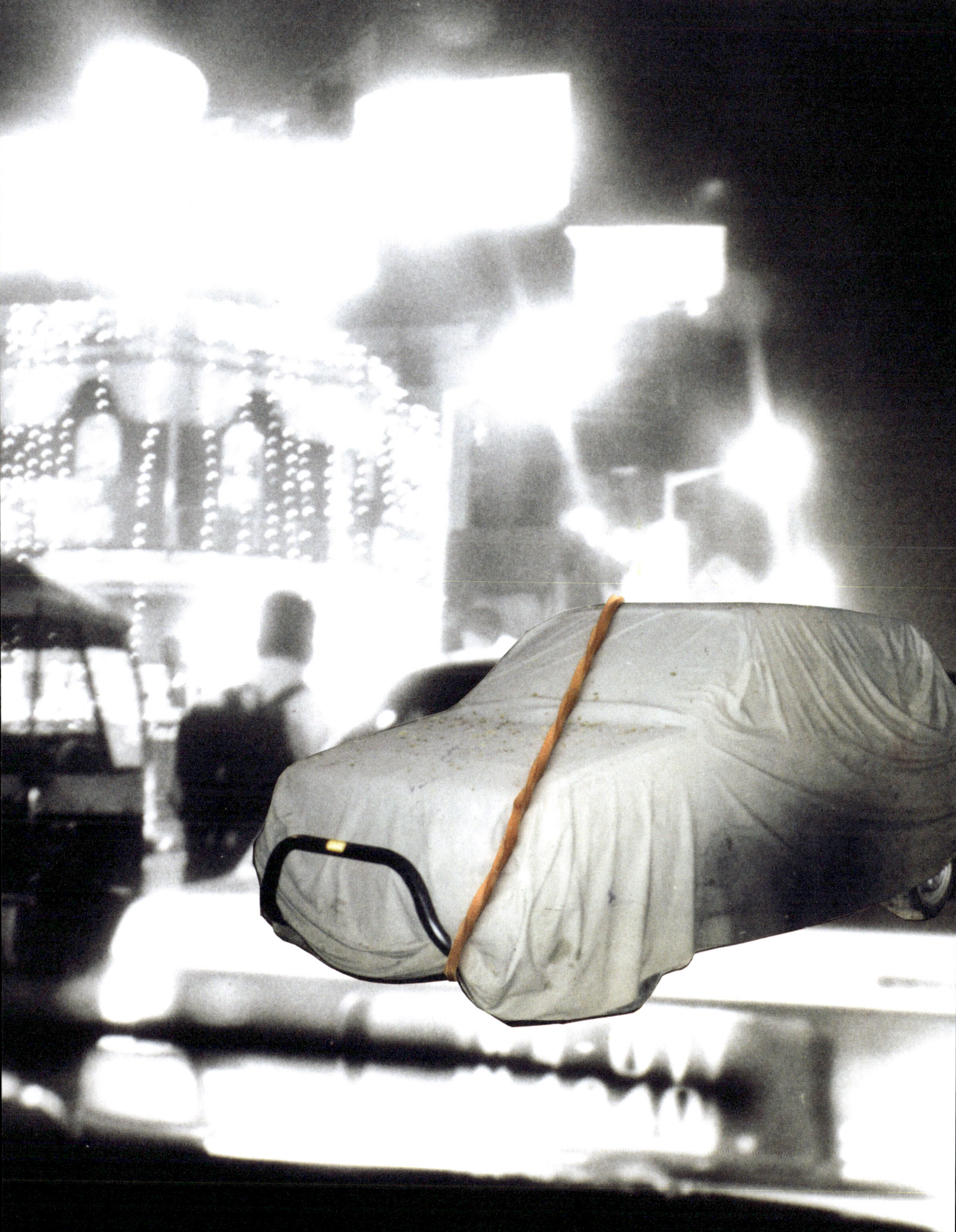

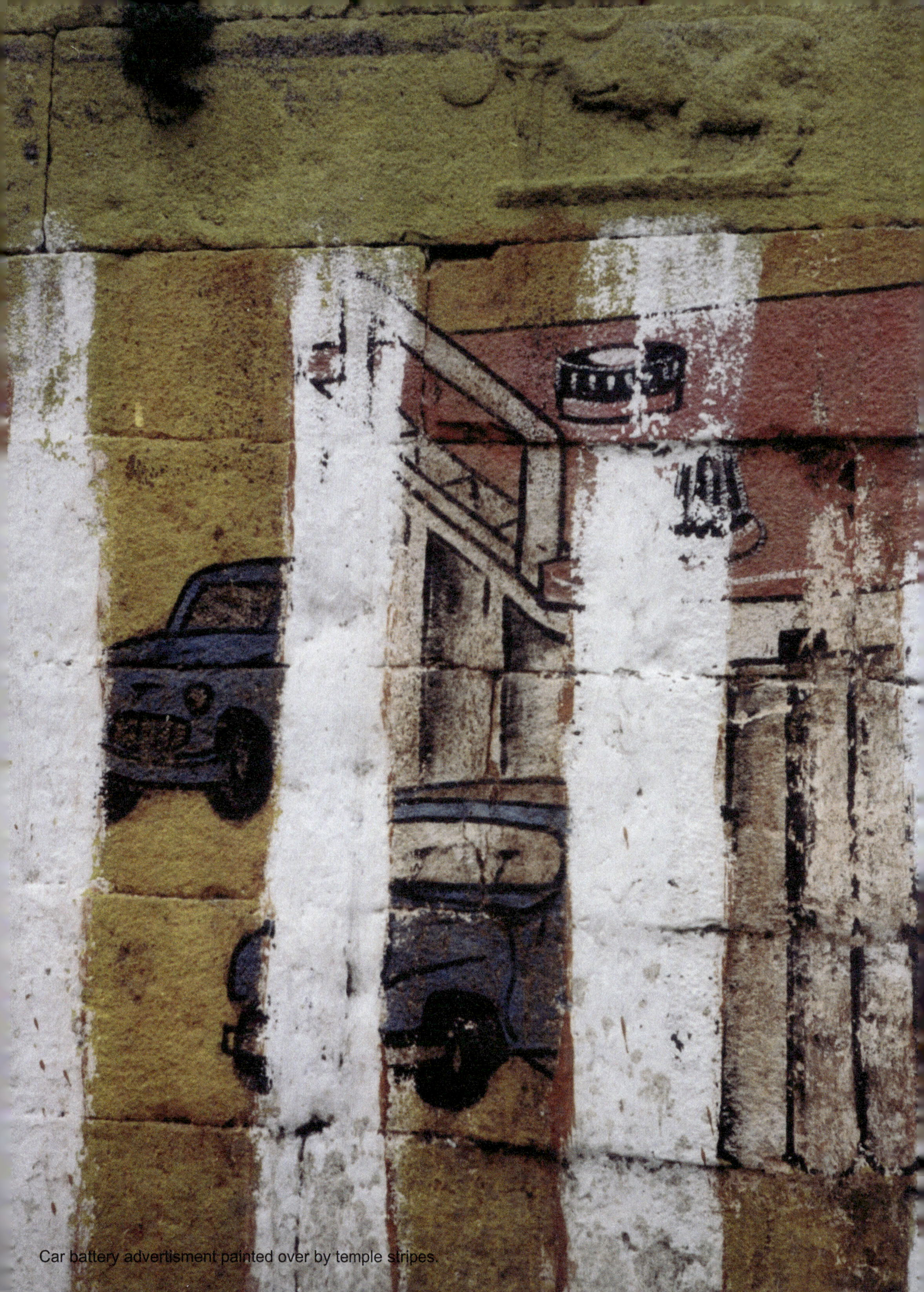

Car battery advertisment painted over by temple stripes.

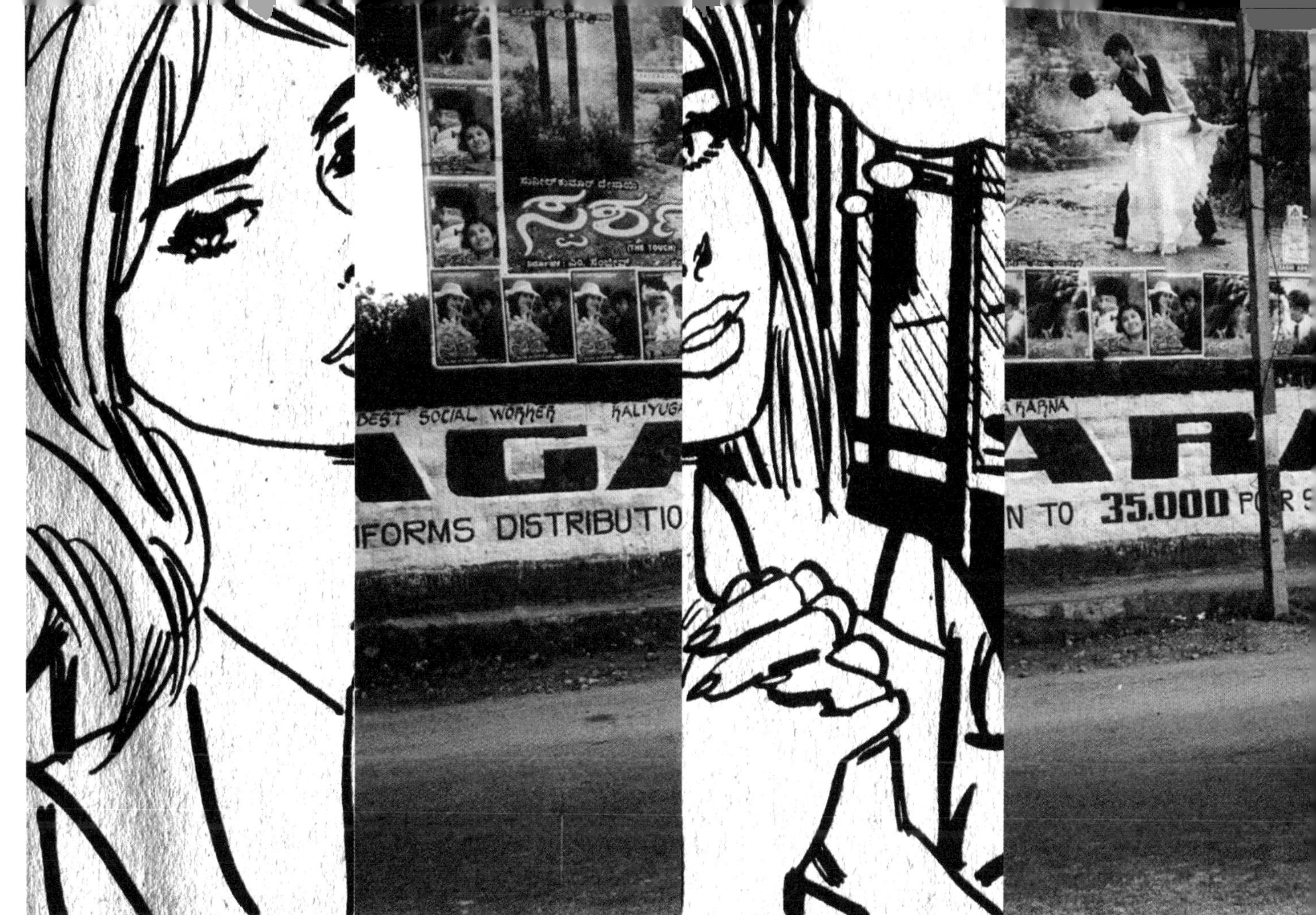
(THE TOUCH)
BEST SOCIAL WORKER
KALIYUGA
KARNA
IFORMS DISTRIBUTIO
N TO 35.000

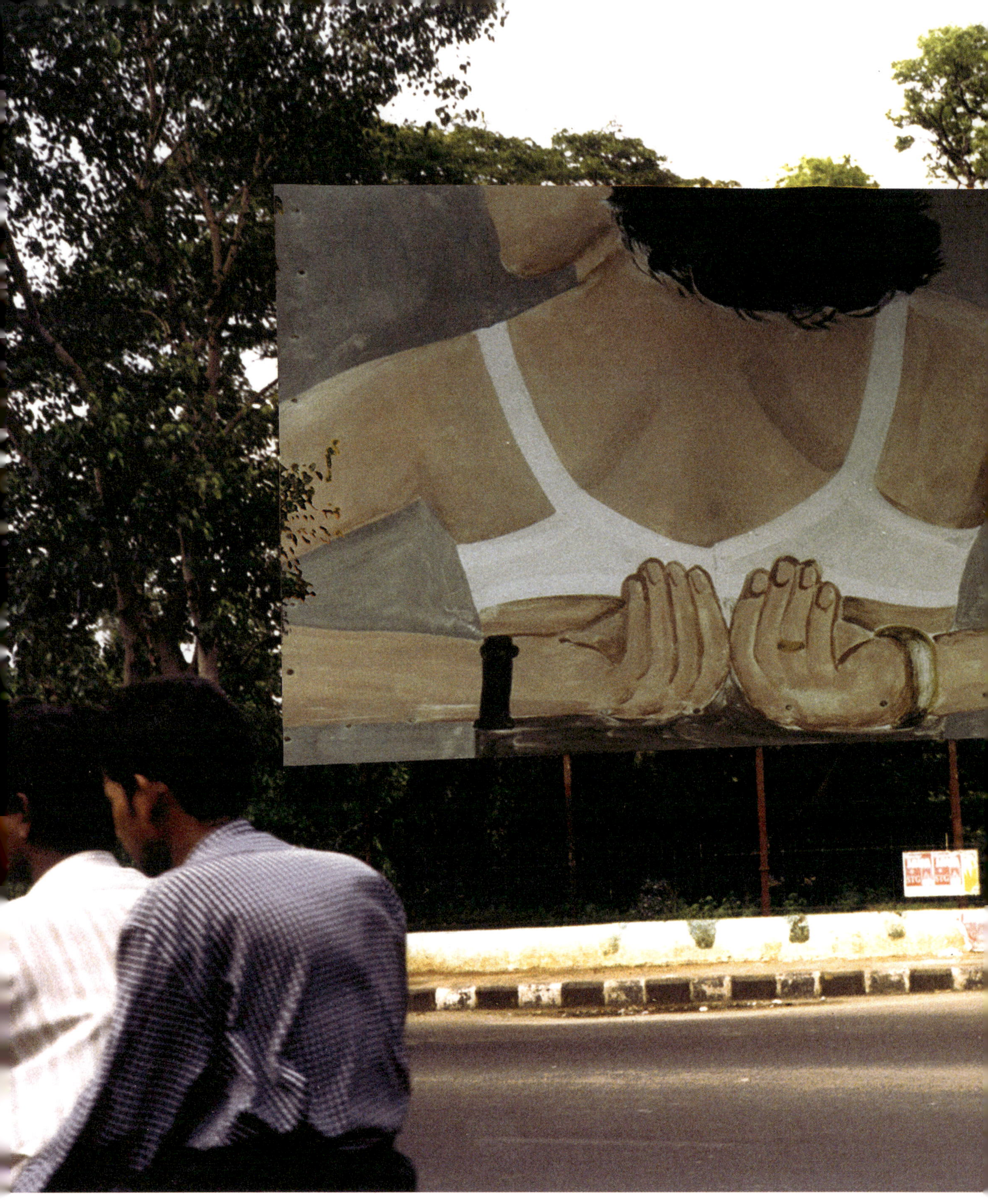

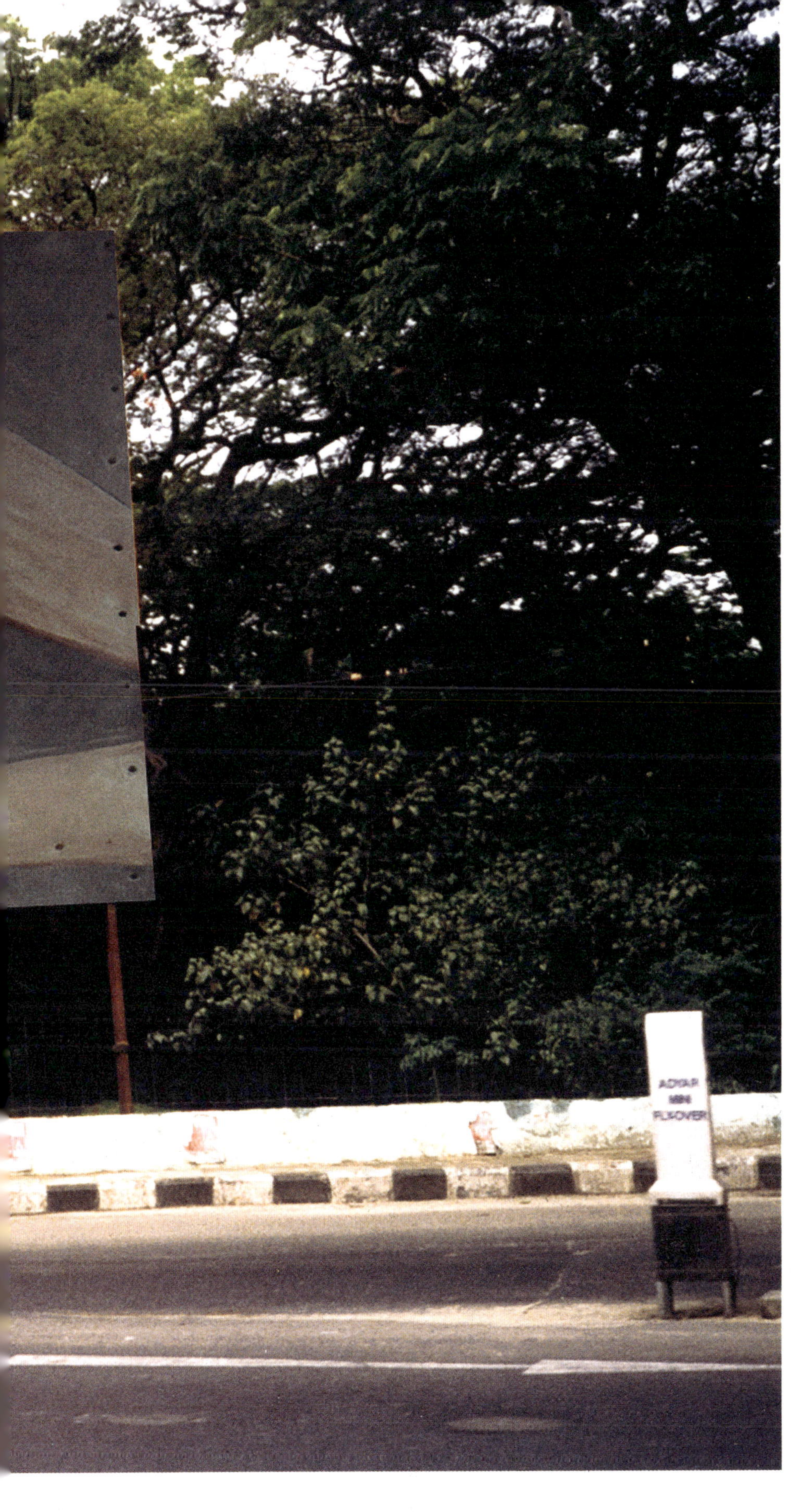
ADYAR
MINI
FLYOVER

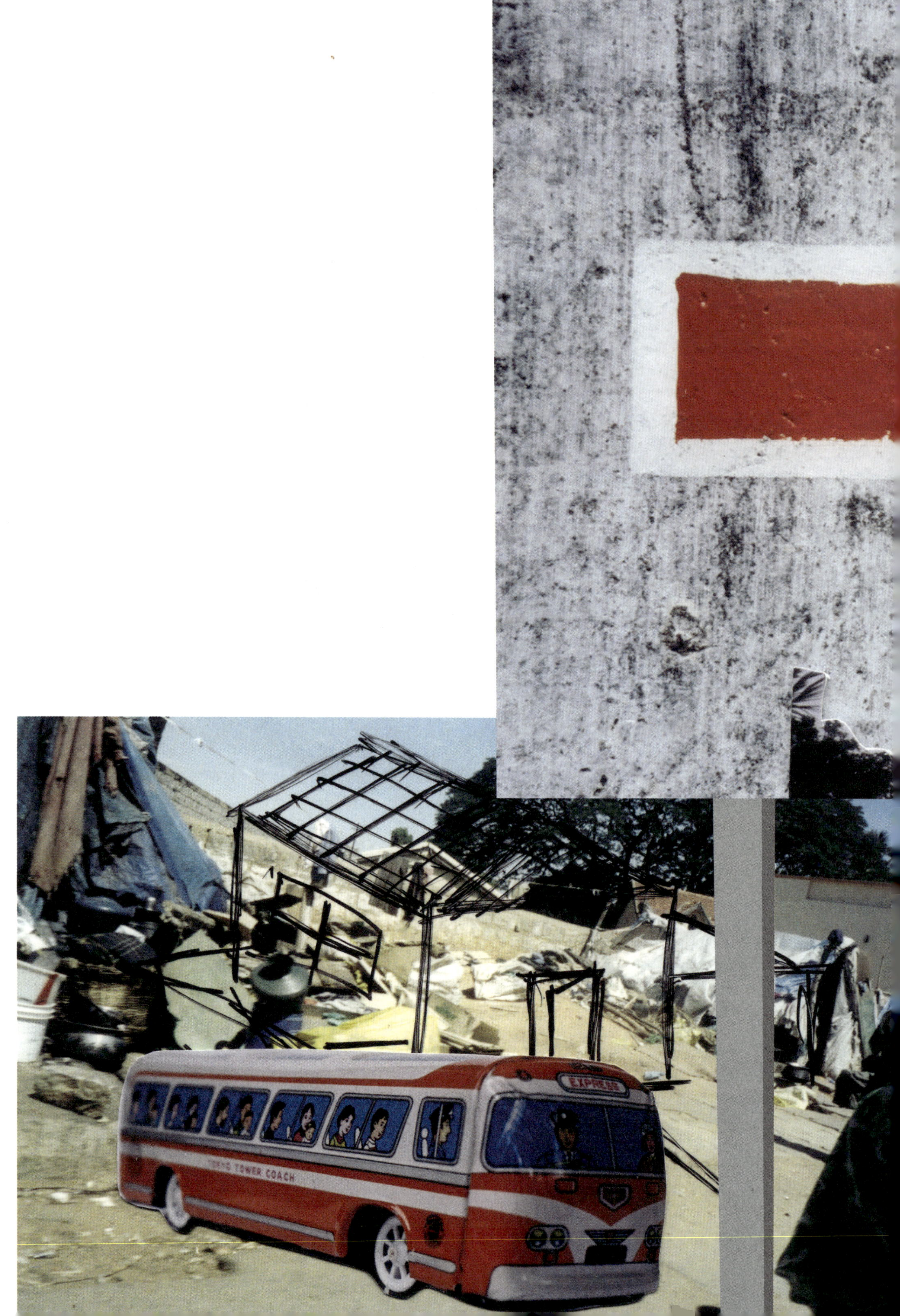
EXPRESS
TOKYO TOWER COACH

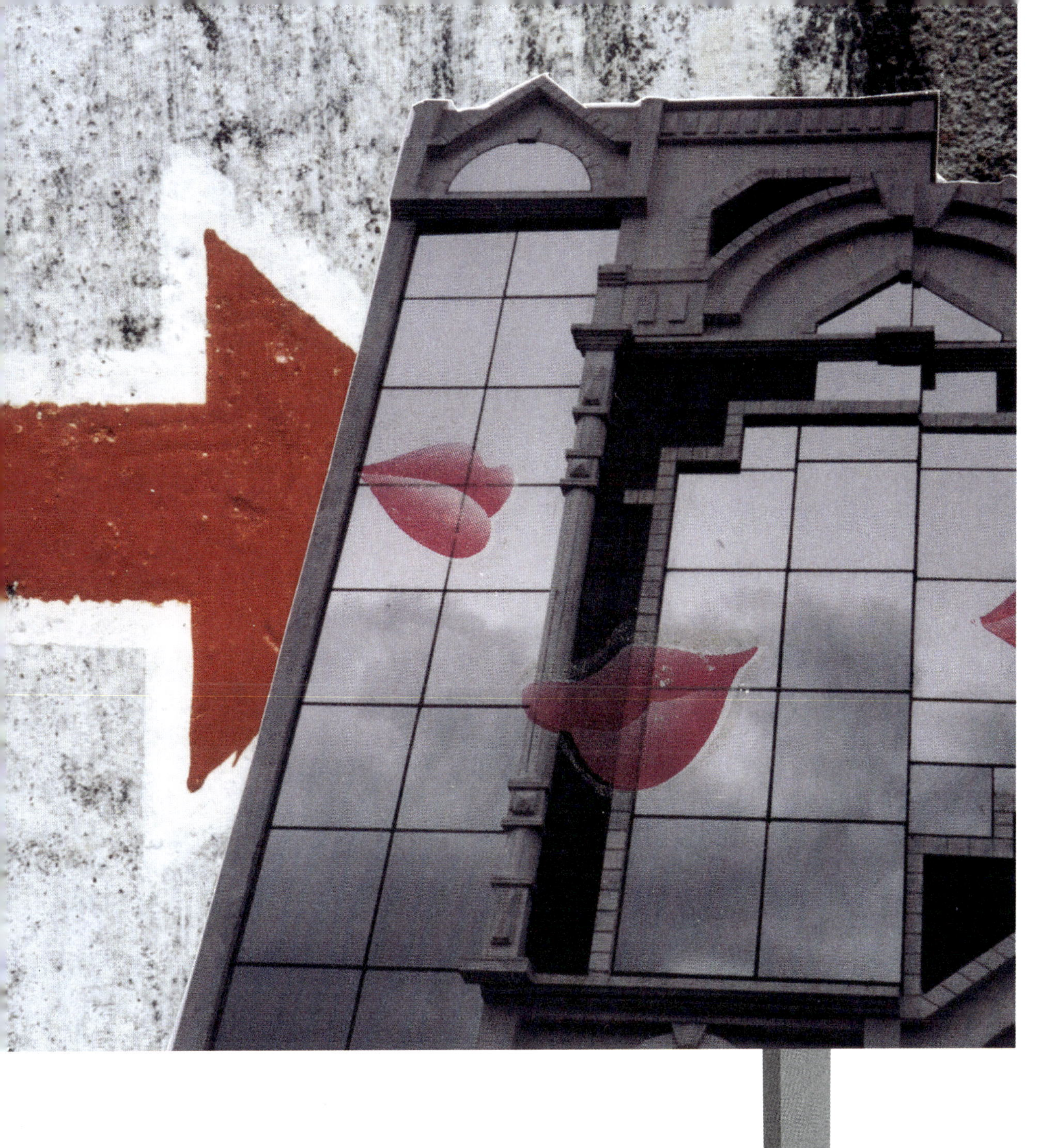

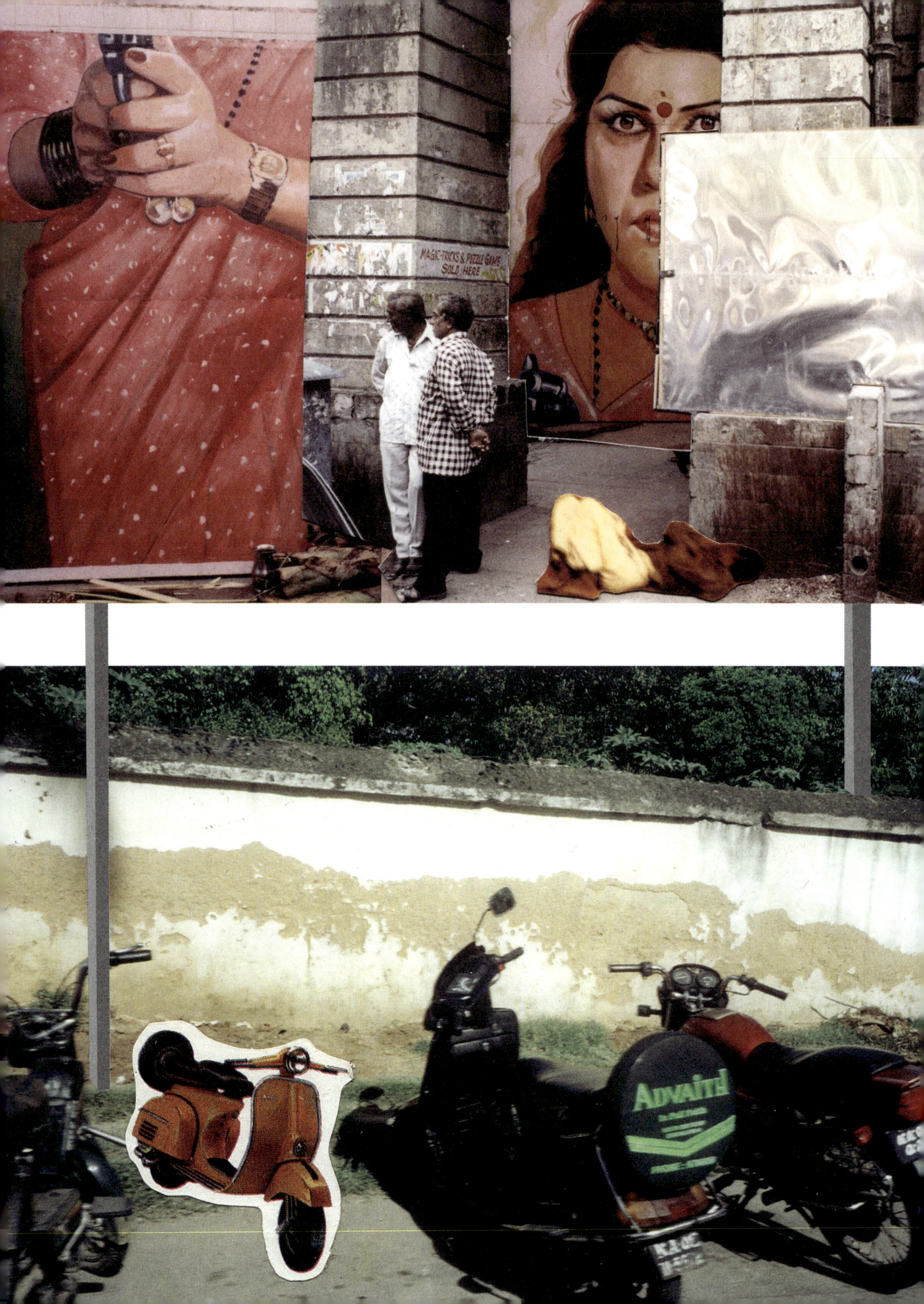
MAGIC-TRICKS & PUZZLE GAME
SOLD HERE

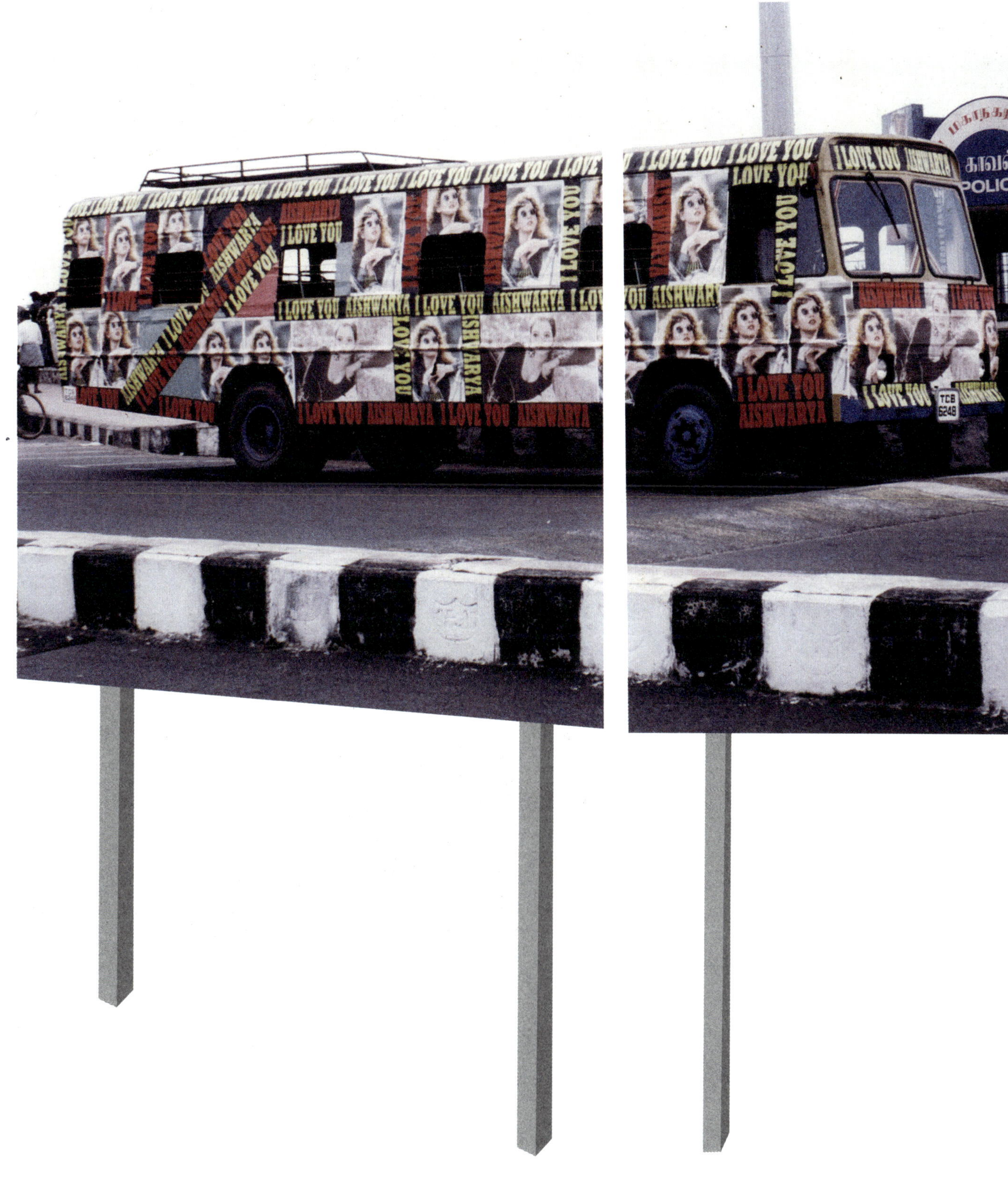
I LOVE YOU
AISHWARYA
காவல்
POLICE
TCB 6248

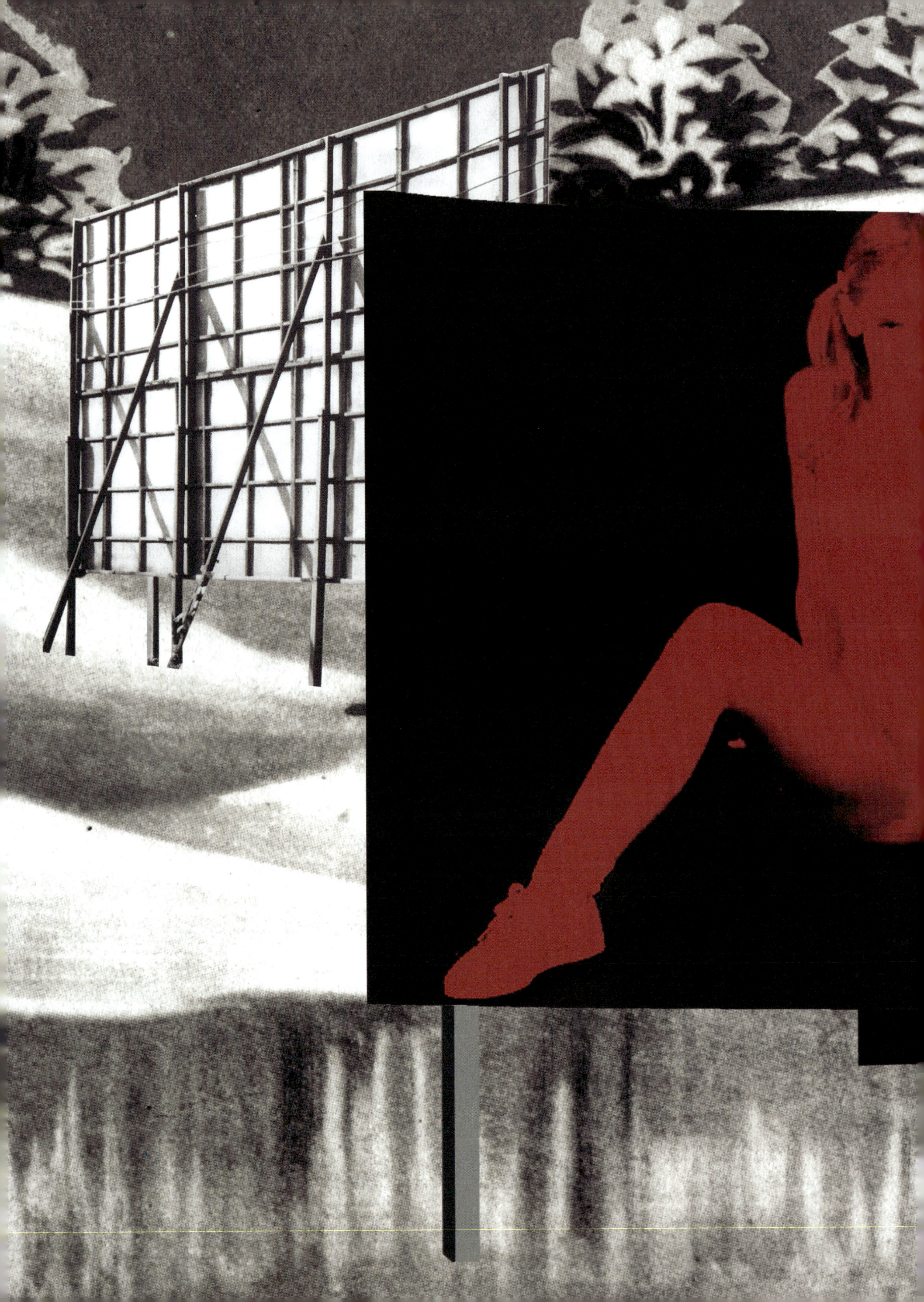

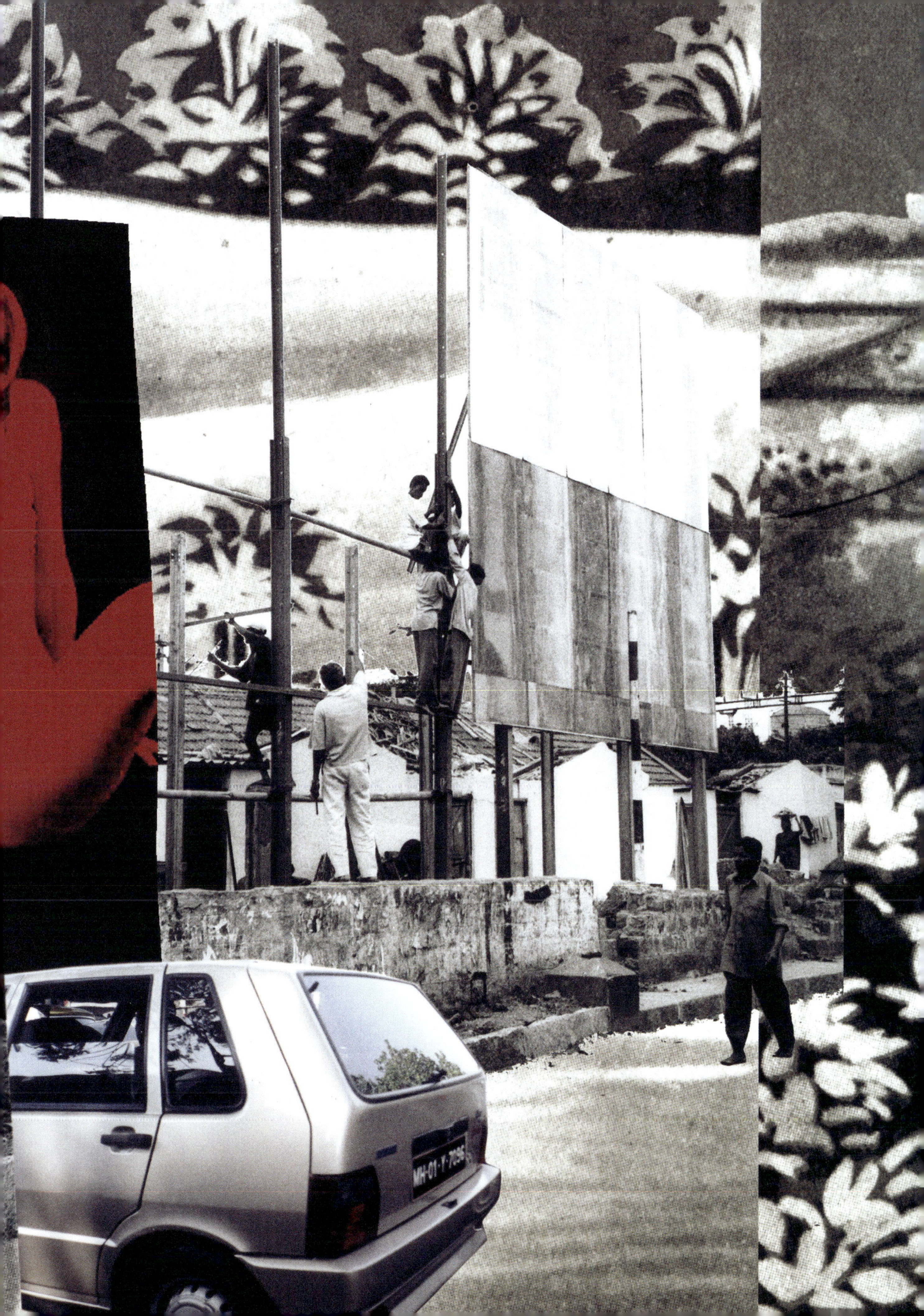

FOI

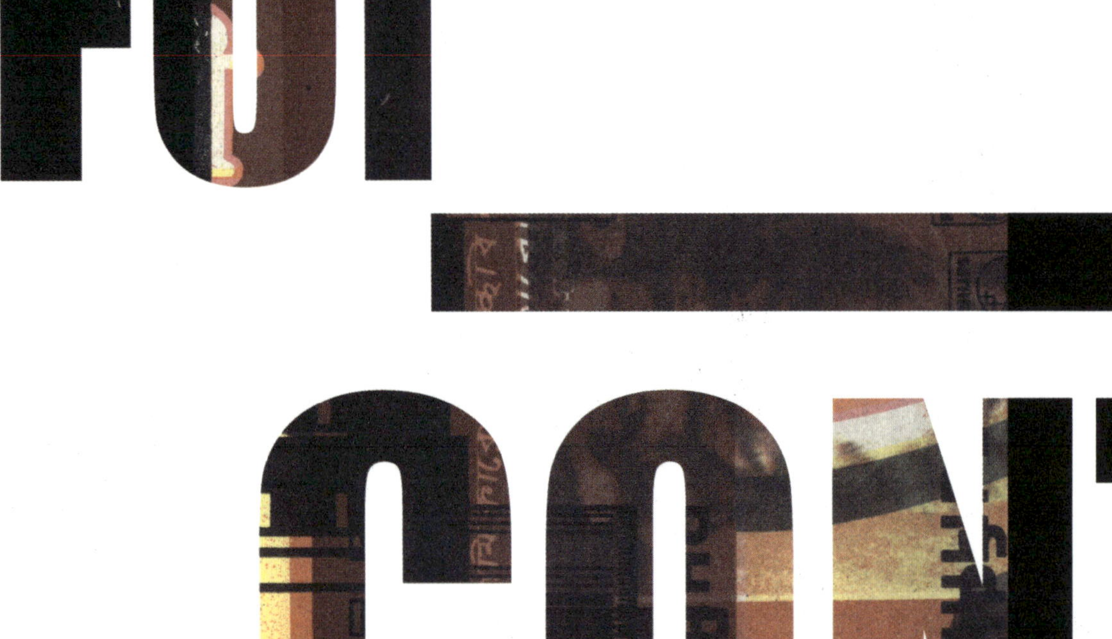

CONT

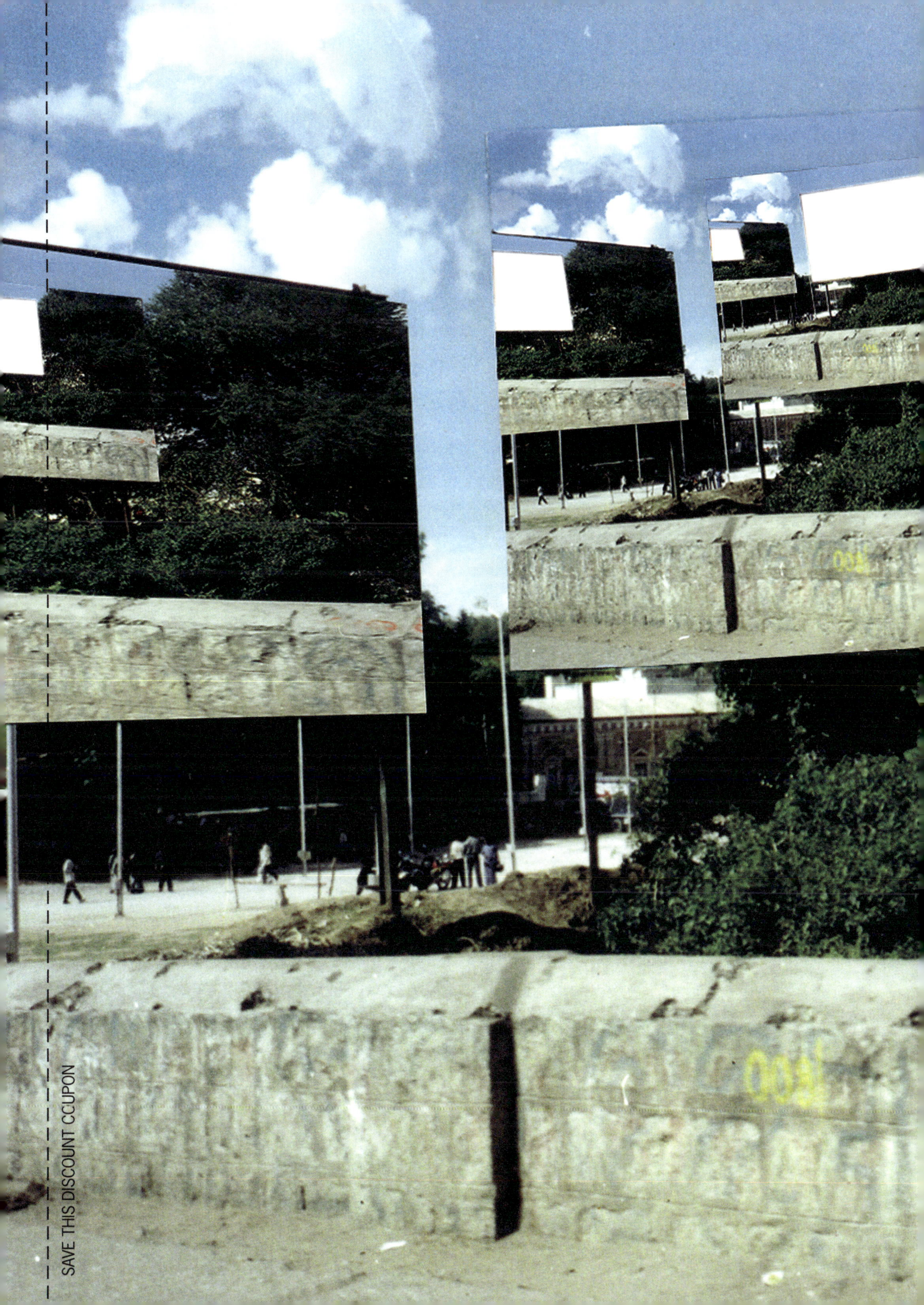
SAVE THIS DISCOUNT CCUPON

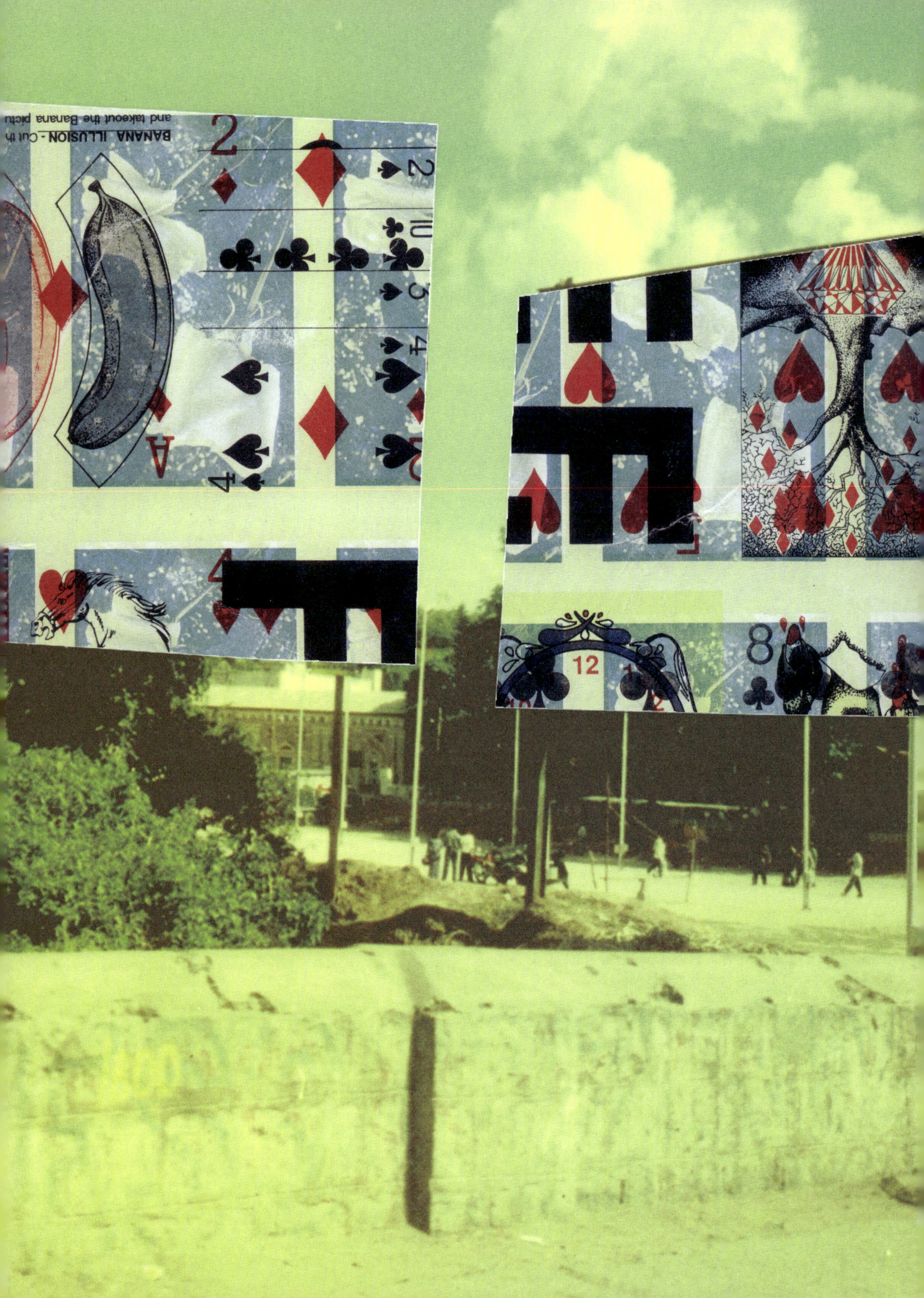
BANANA ILLUSION - Cut th
and takeout the Banana pictu

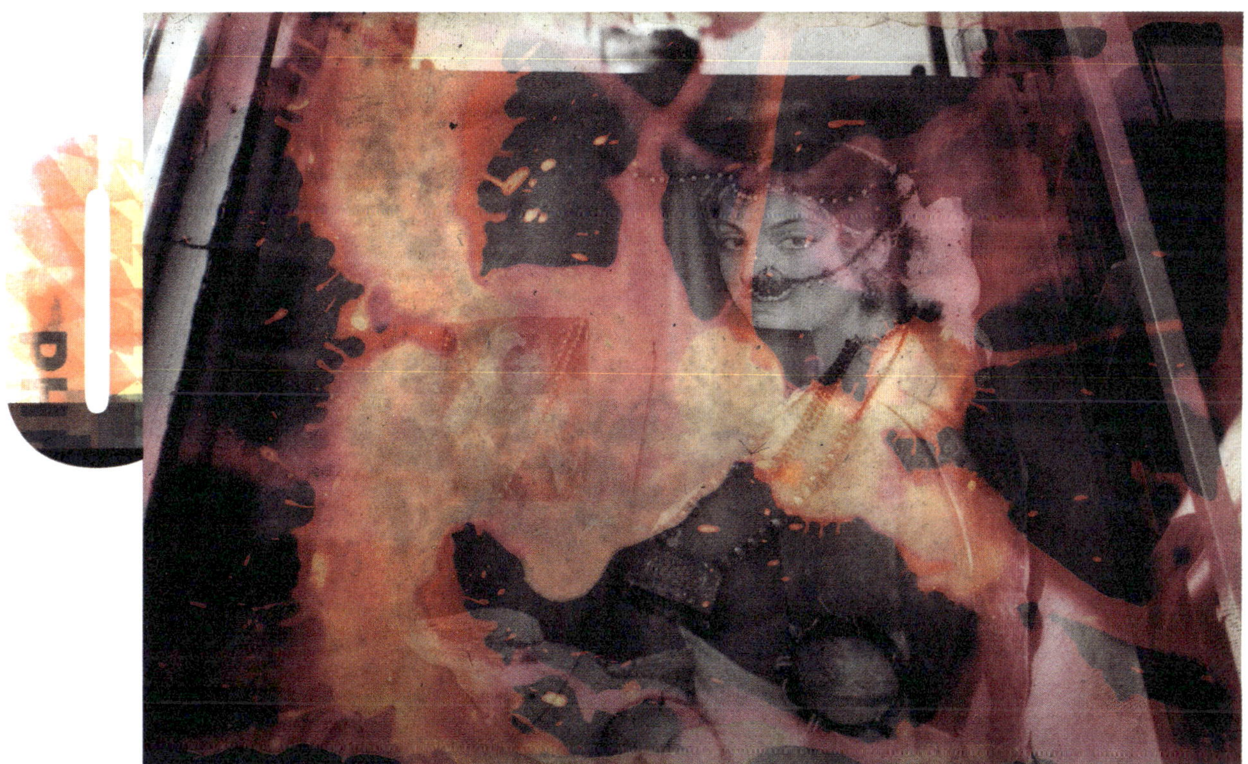

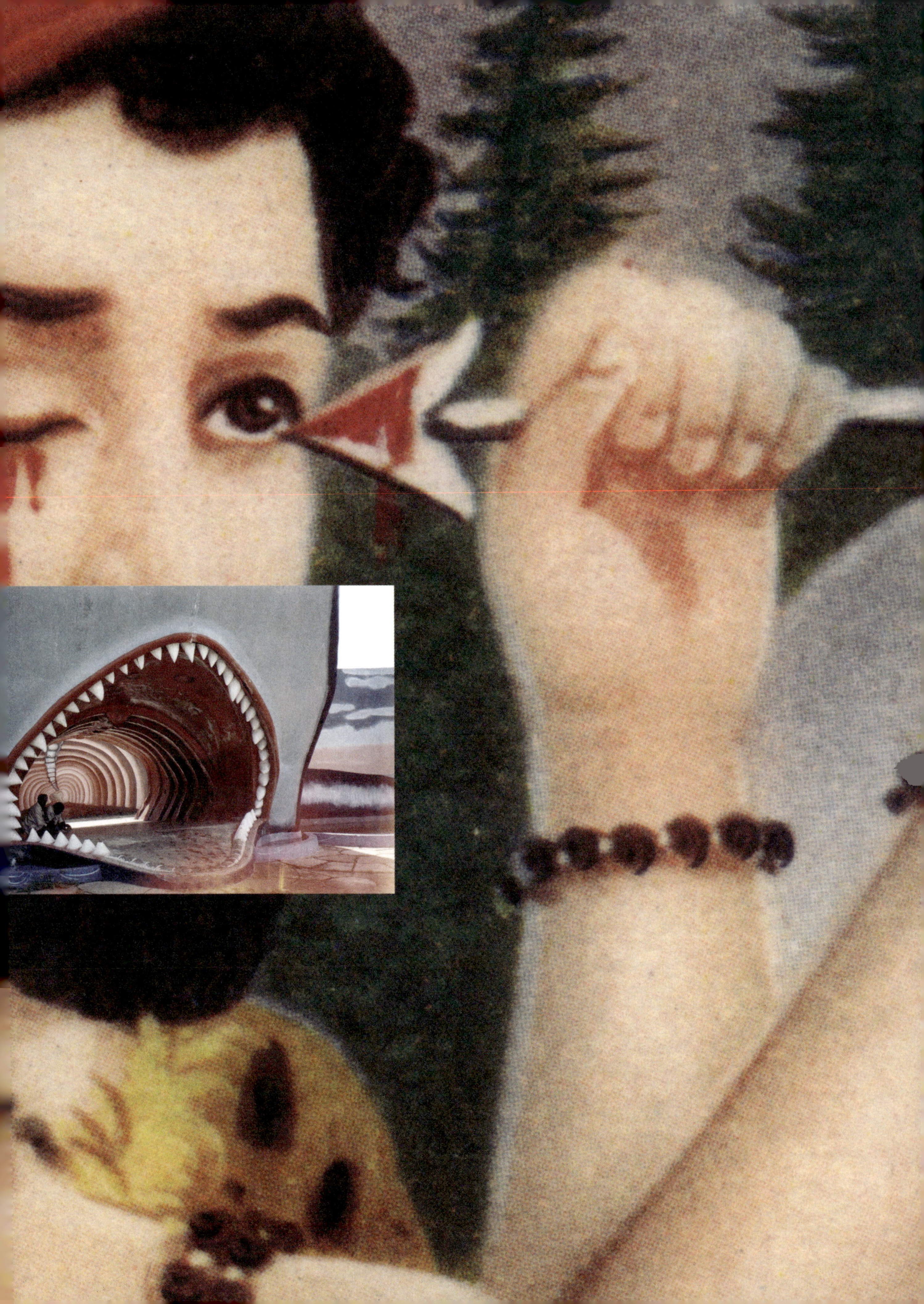

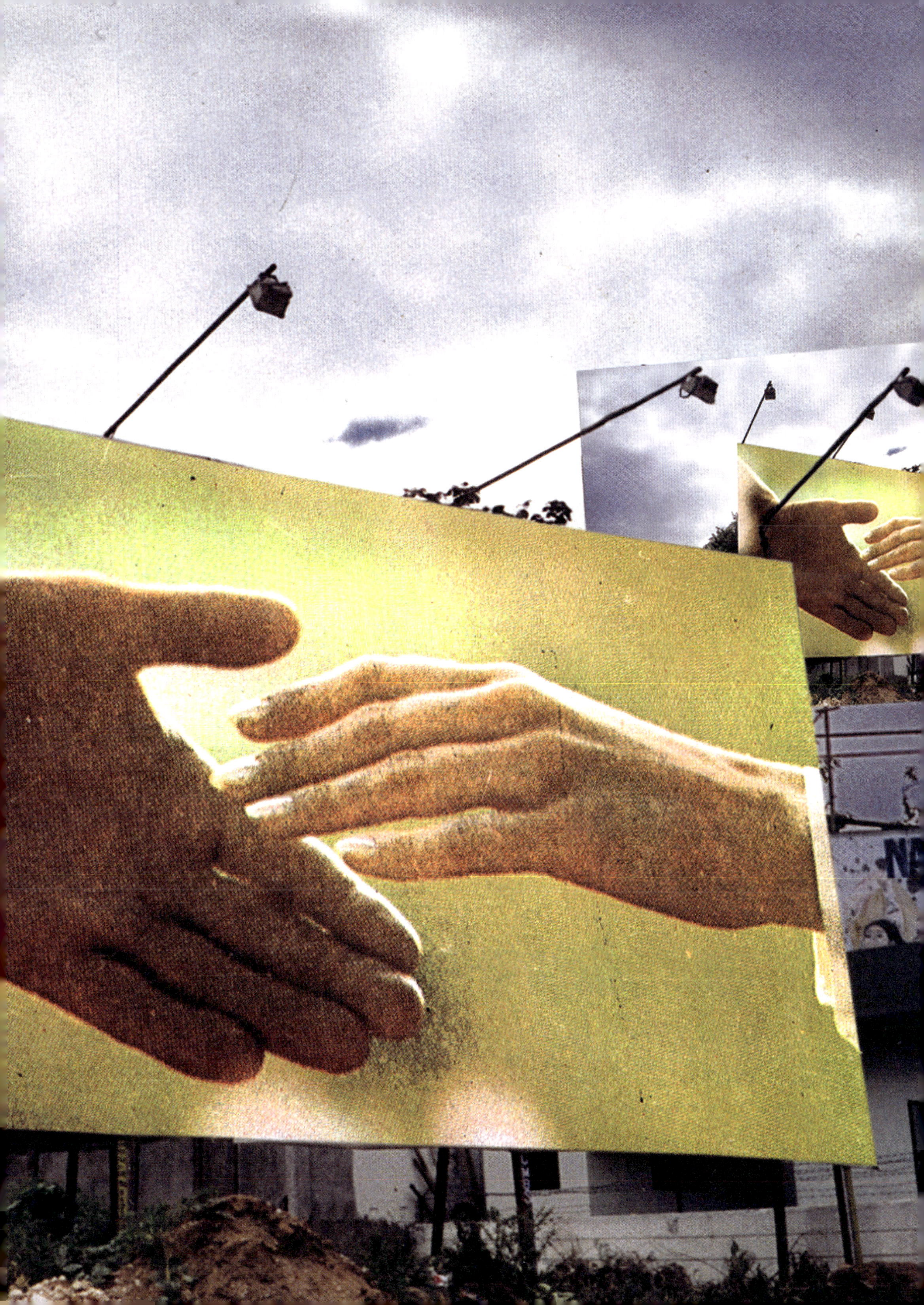

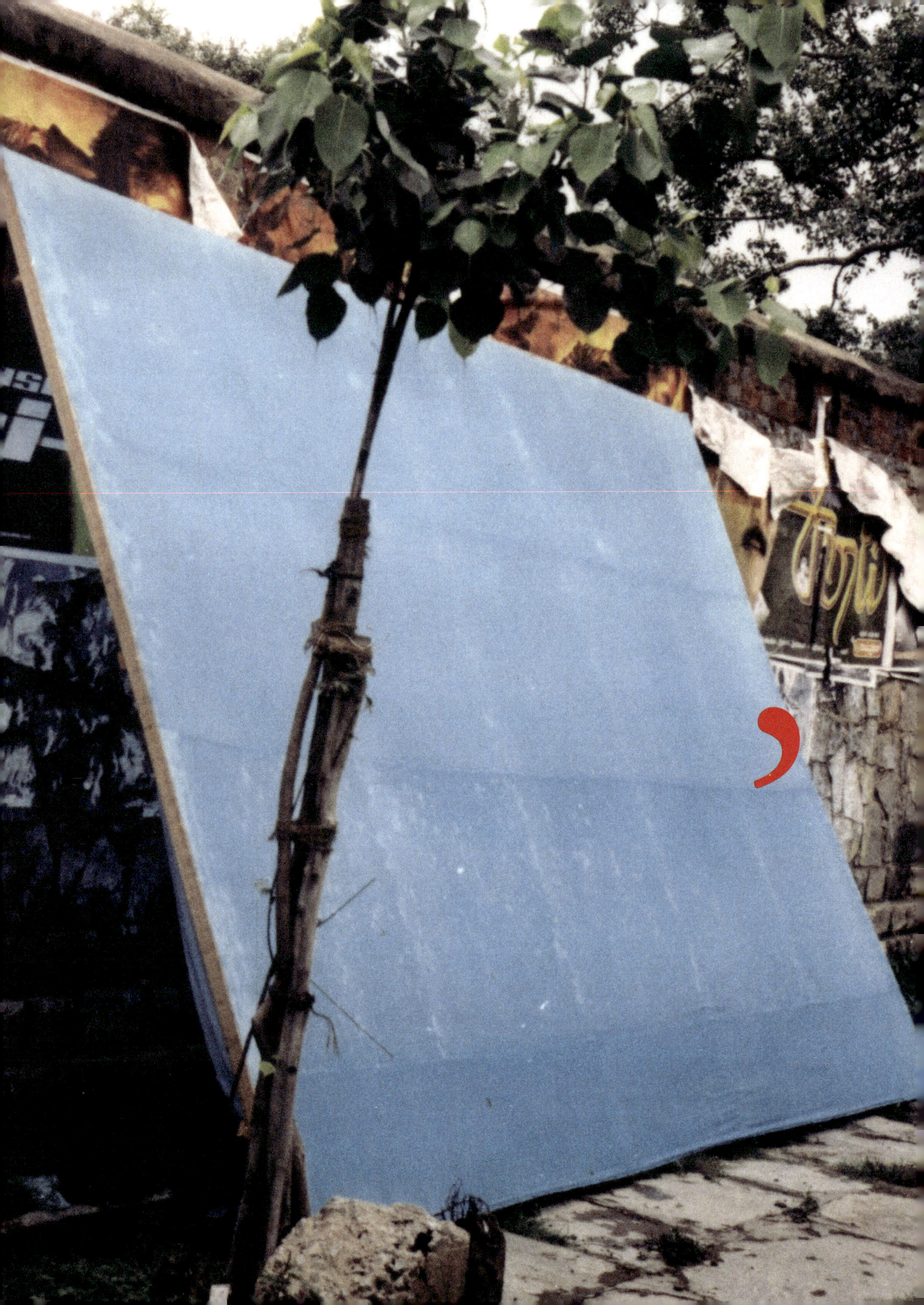

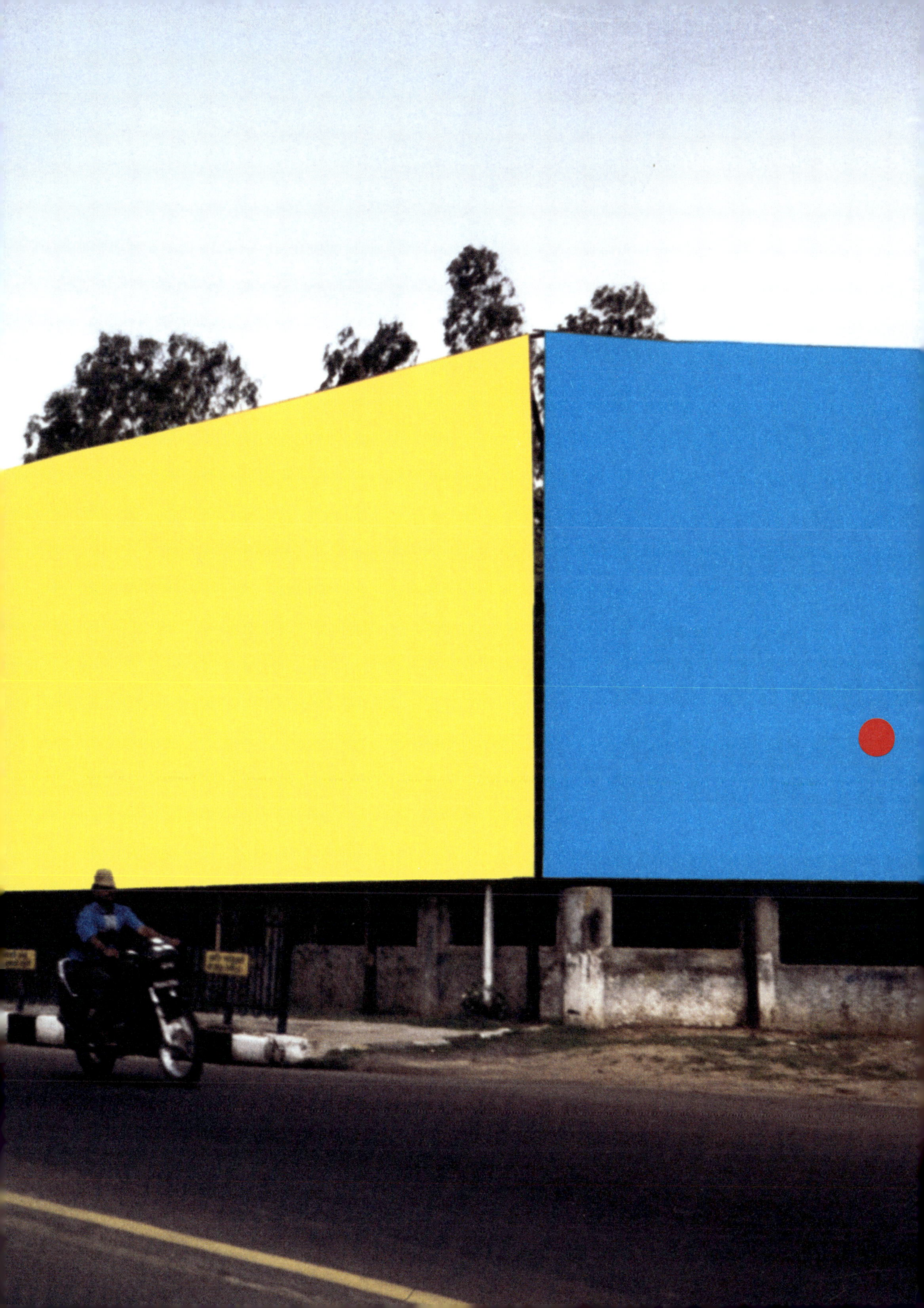

Weak Architecture

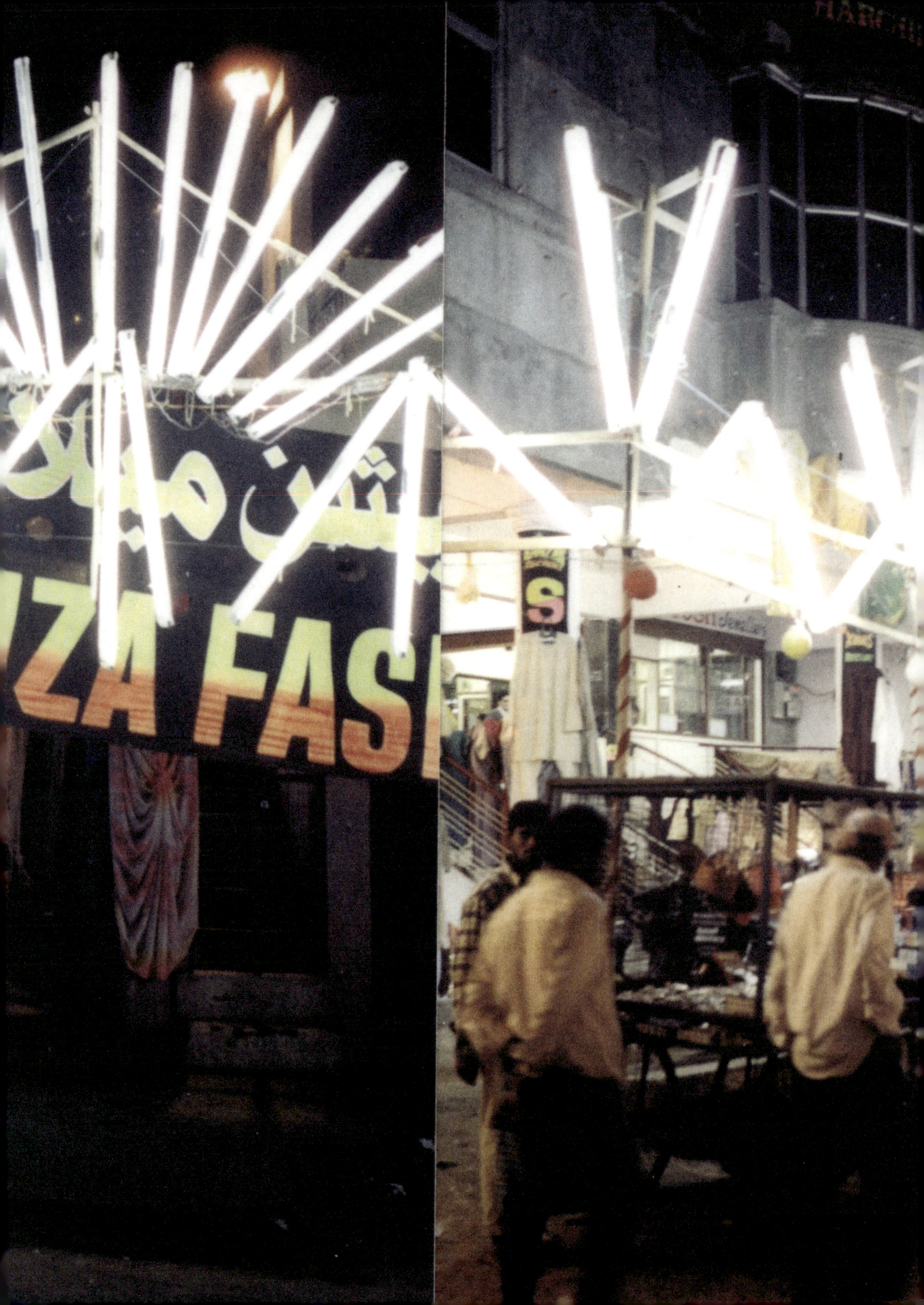
ZA FAS
S

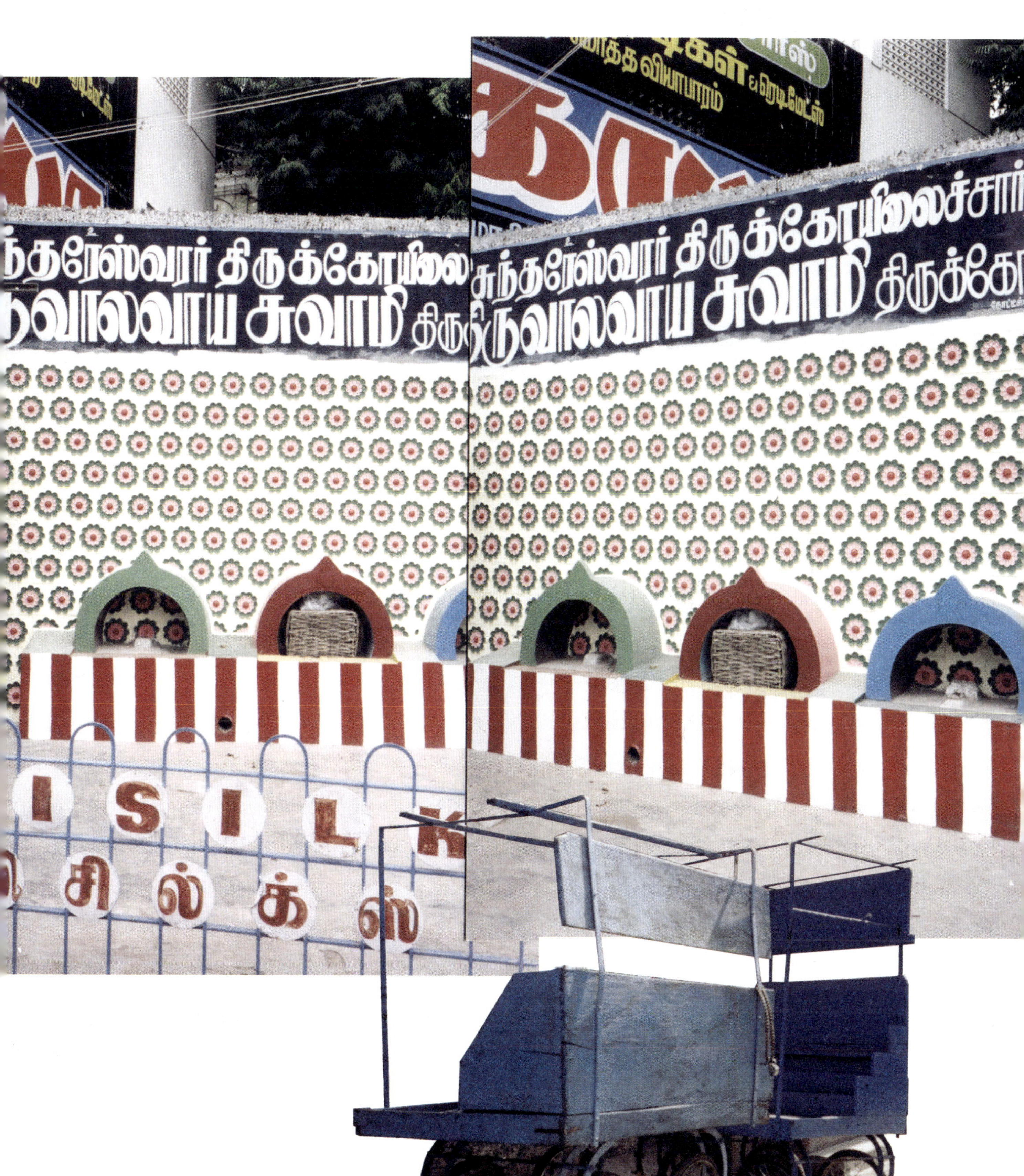
மொத்த வியாபாரம்
ரெடிமேட்ஸ்
ந்தரேஸ்வரர் திருக்கோயிலை
ருவாலவாய சுவாமி திரு
சுந்தரேஸ்வரர் திருக்கோயிலைச்சார்
ருவாலவாய சுவாமி திருக்கோ
S I L
சில்க்ஸ்

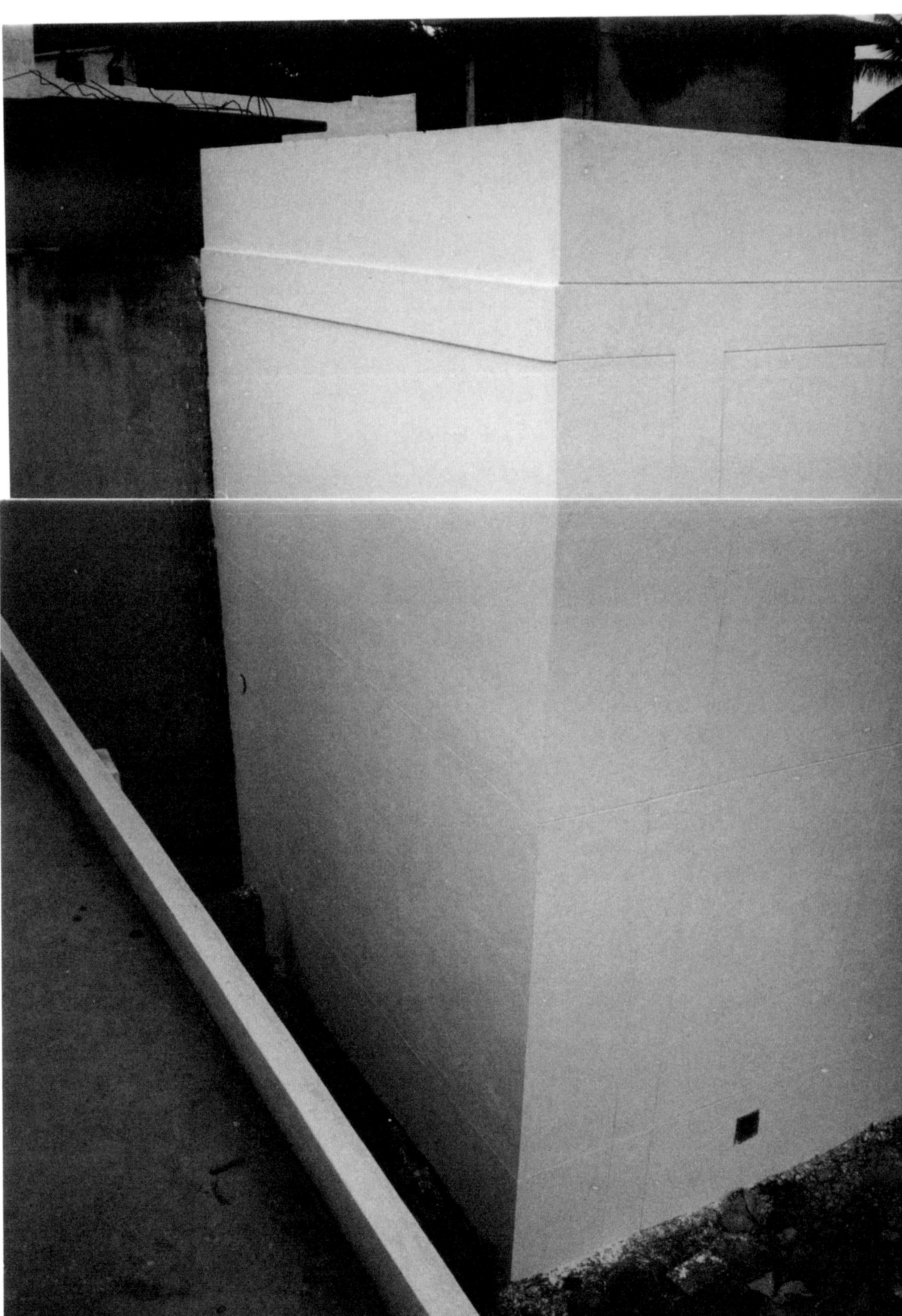

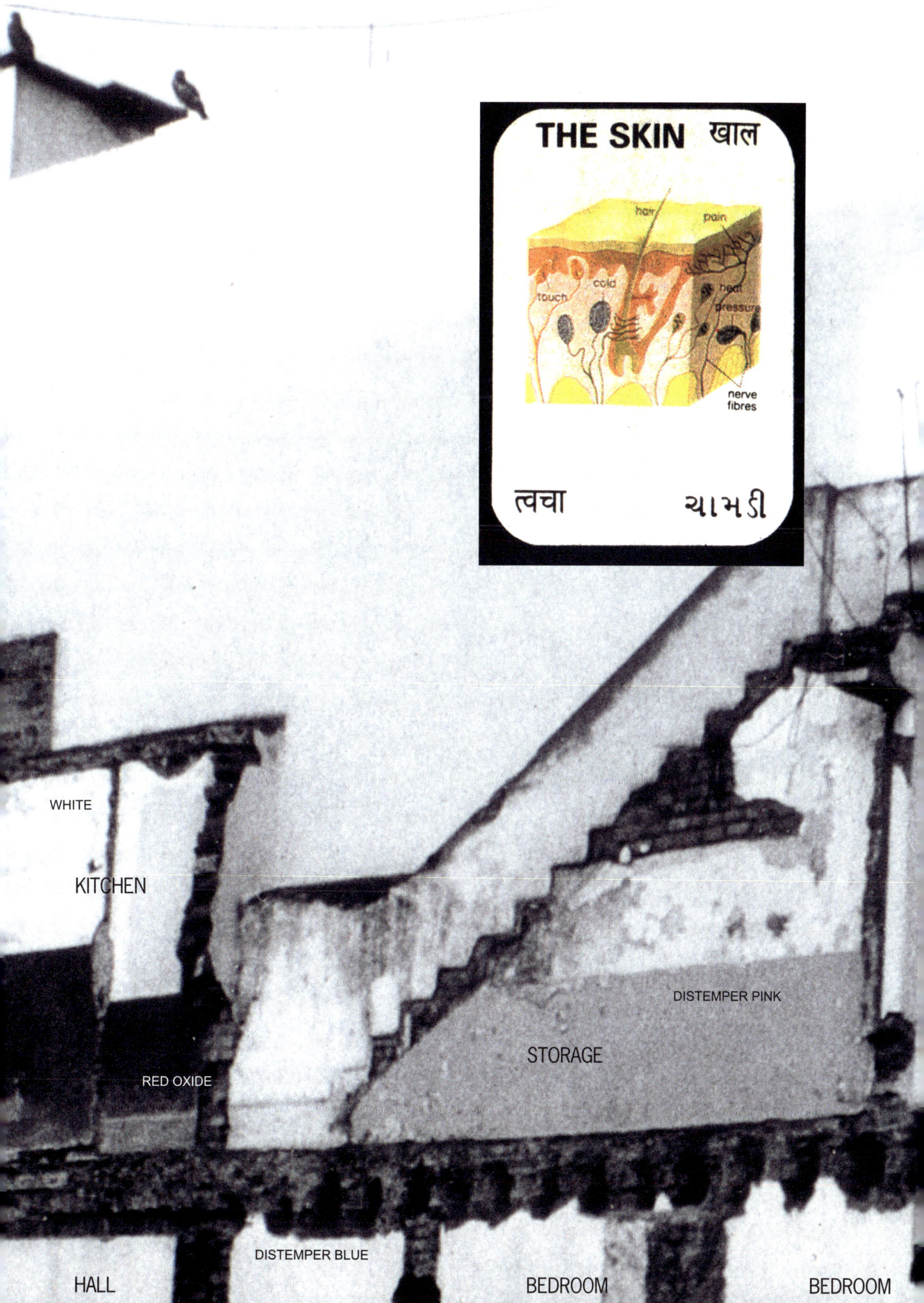

THE SKIN खाल
hair
pain
touch
cold
heat
pressure
nerve fibres
त्वचा
ચામડી
WHITE
KITCHEN
RED OXIDE
DISTEMPER PINK
STORAGE
DISTEMPER BLUE
HALL
BEDROOM
BEDROOM

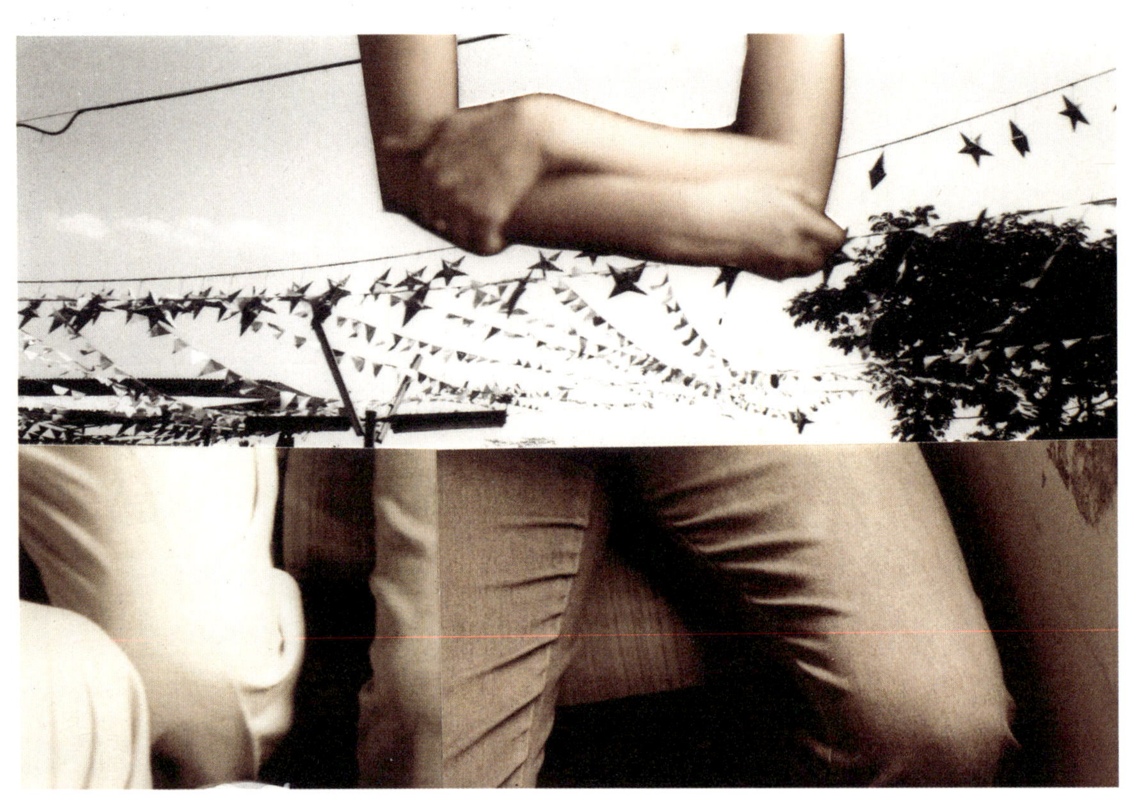

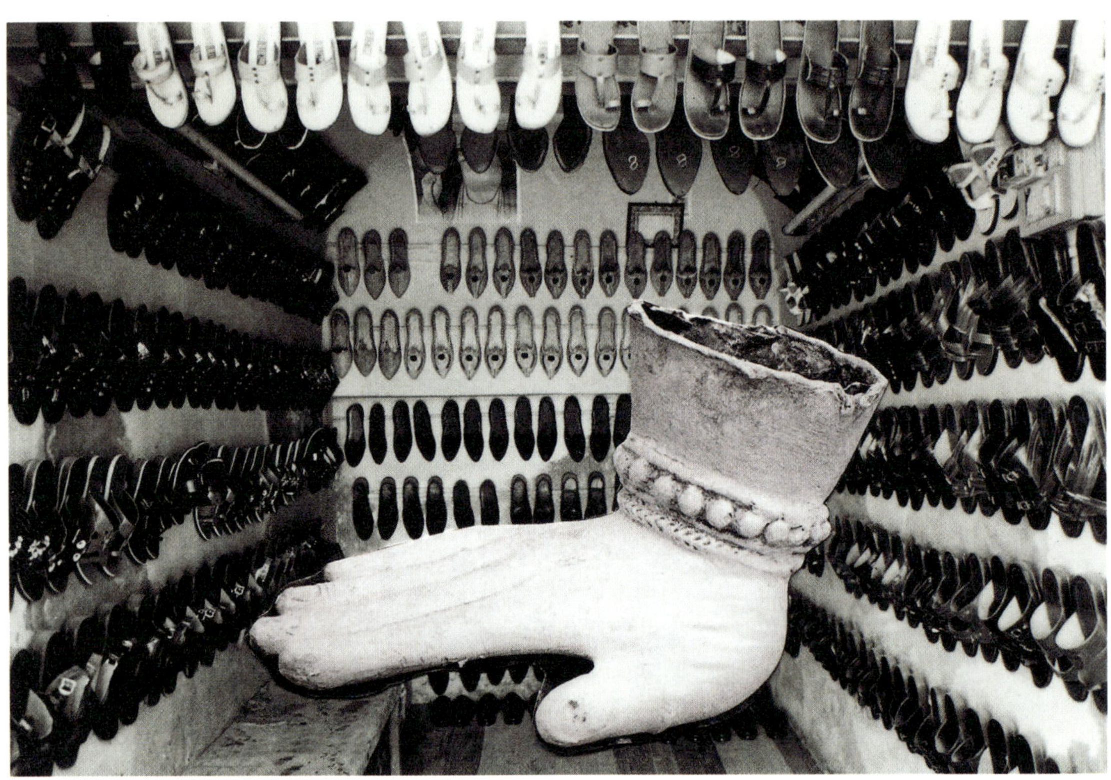

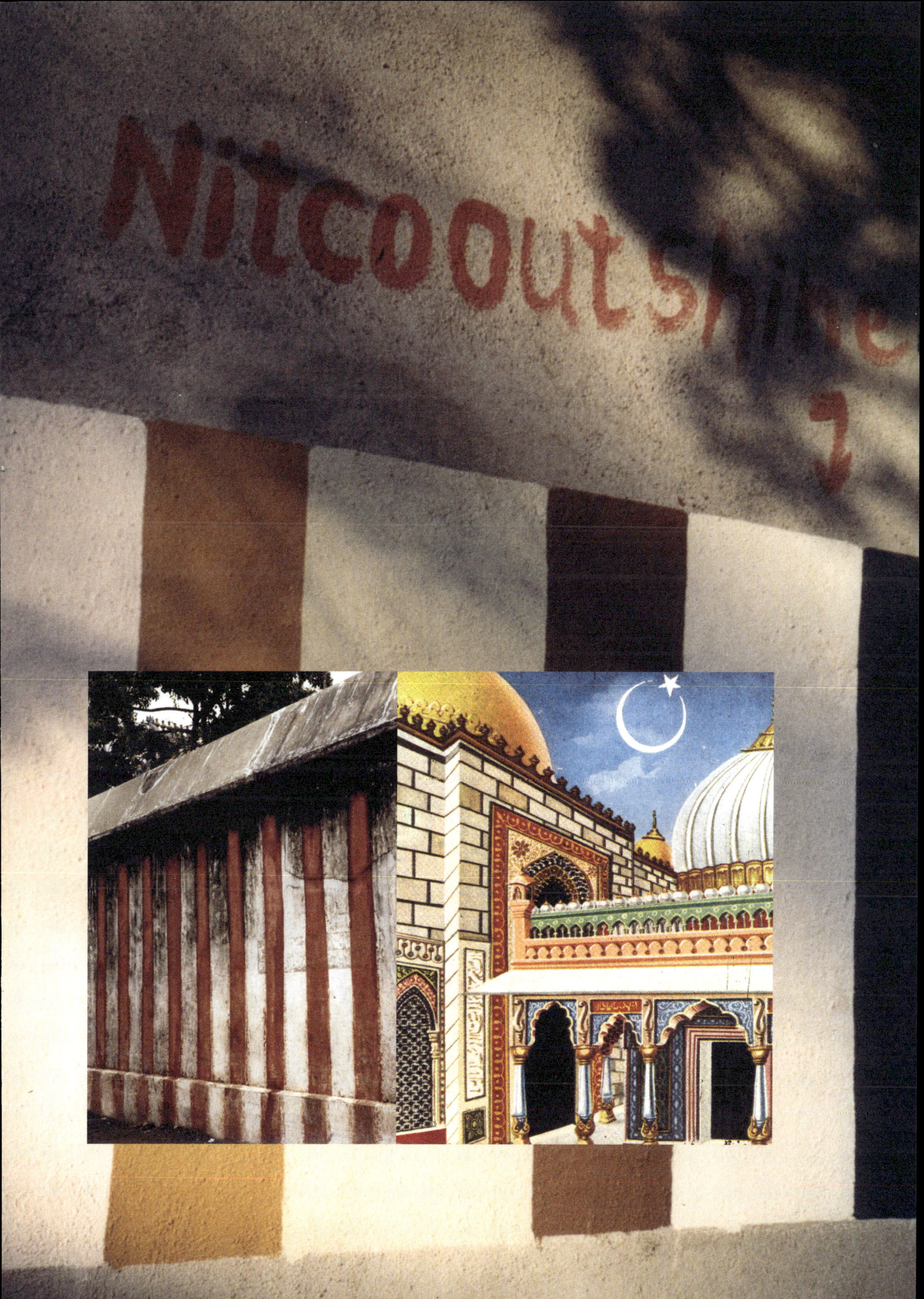
Nitco outshine

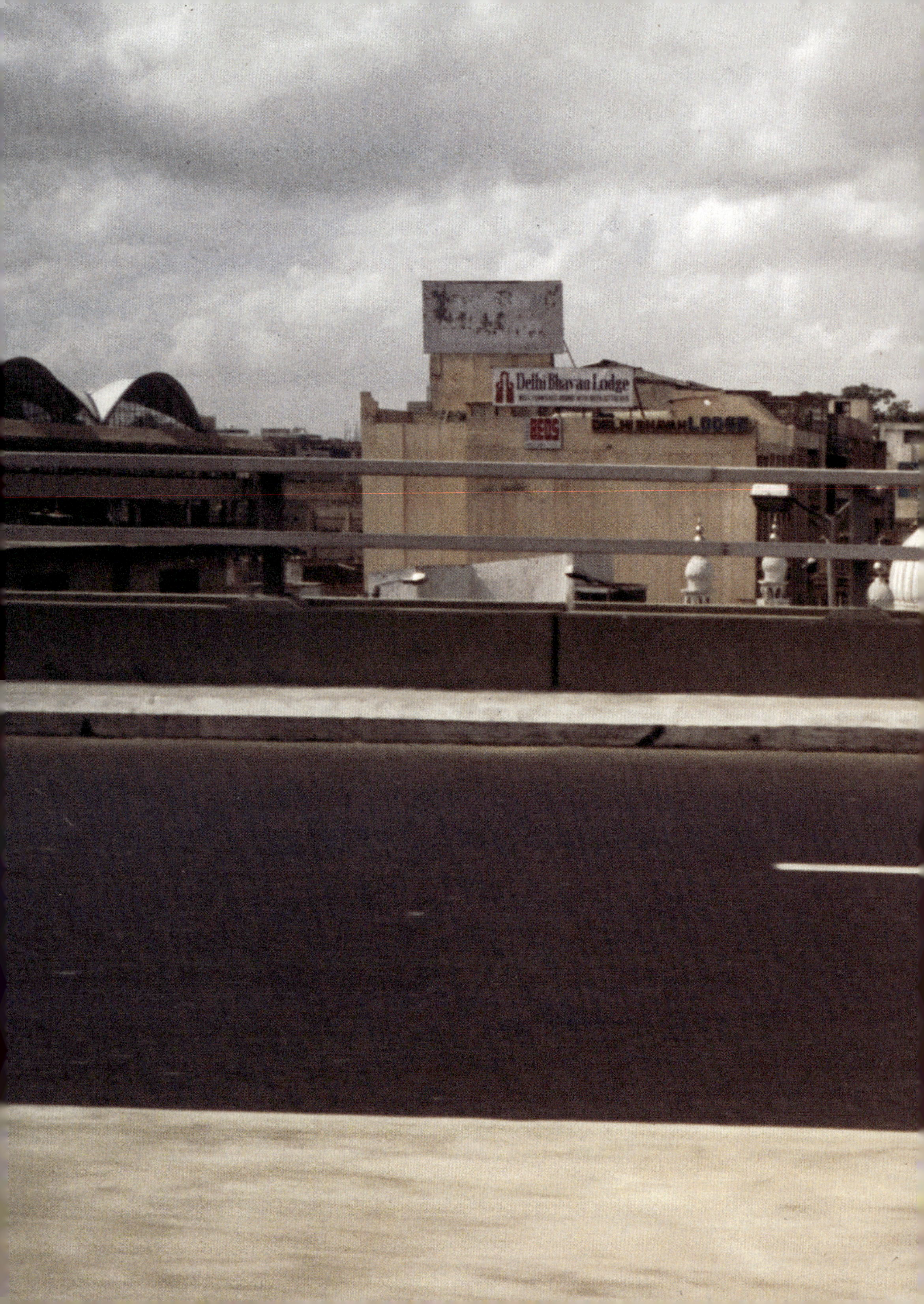
Delhi Bhavan Lodge

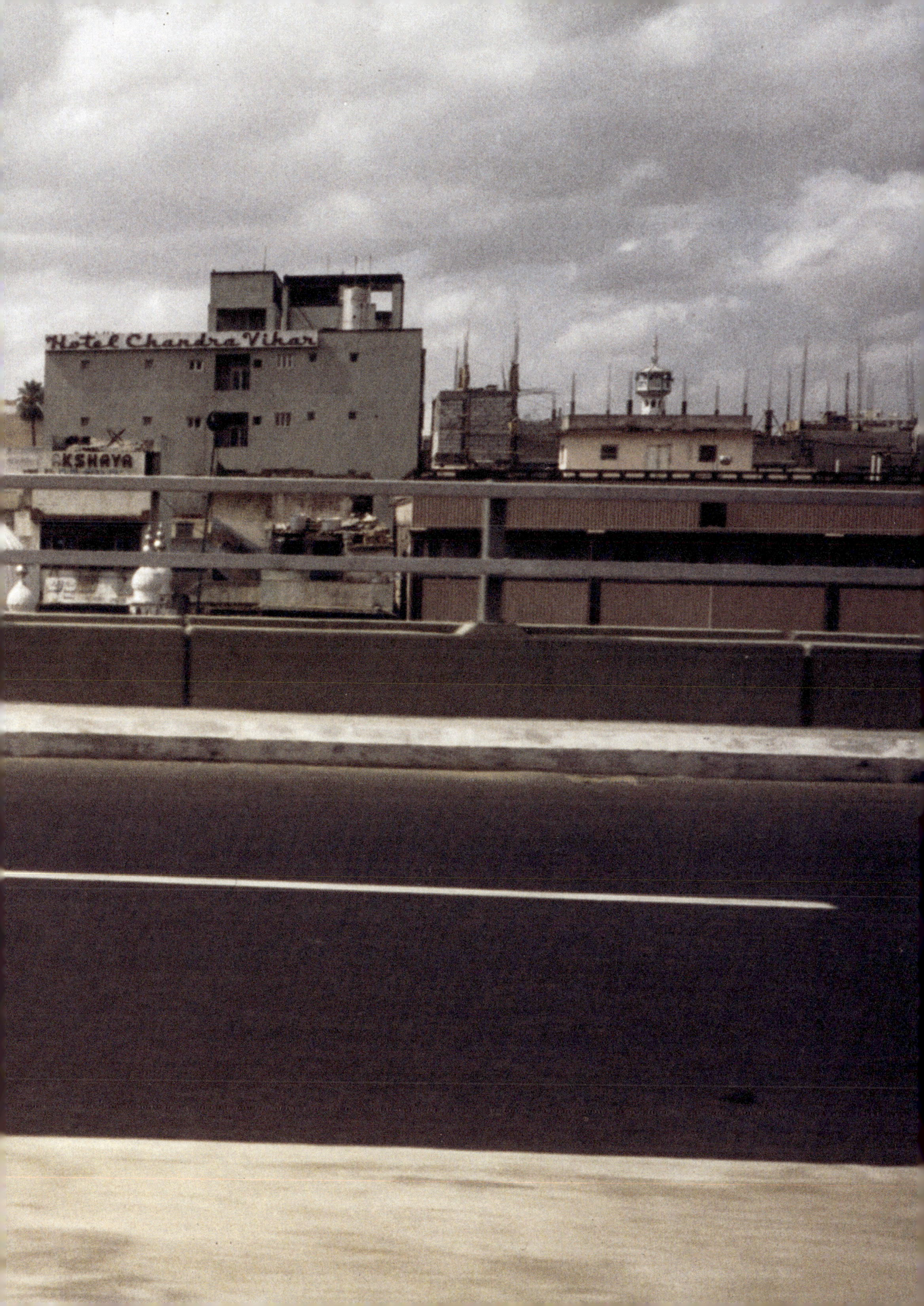
Hotel Chandra Vihar
KSHAYA

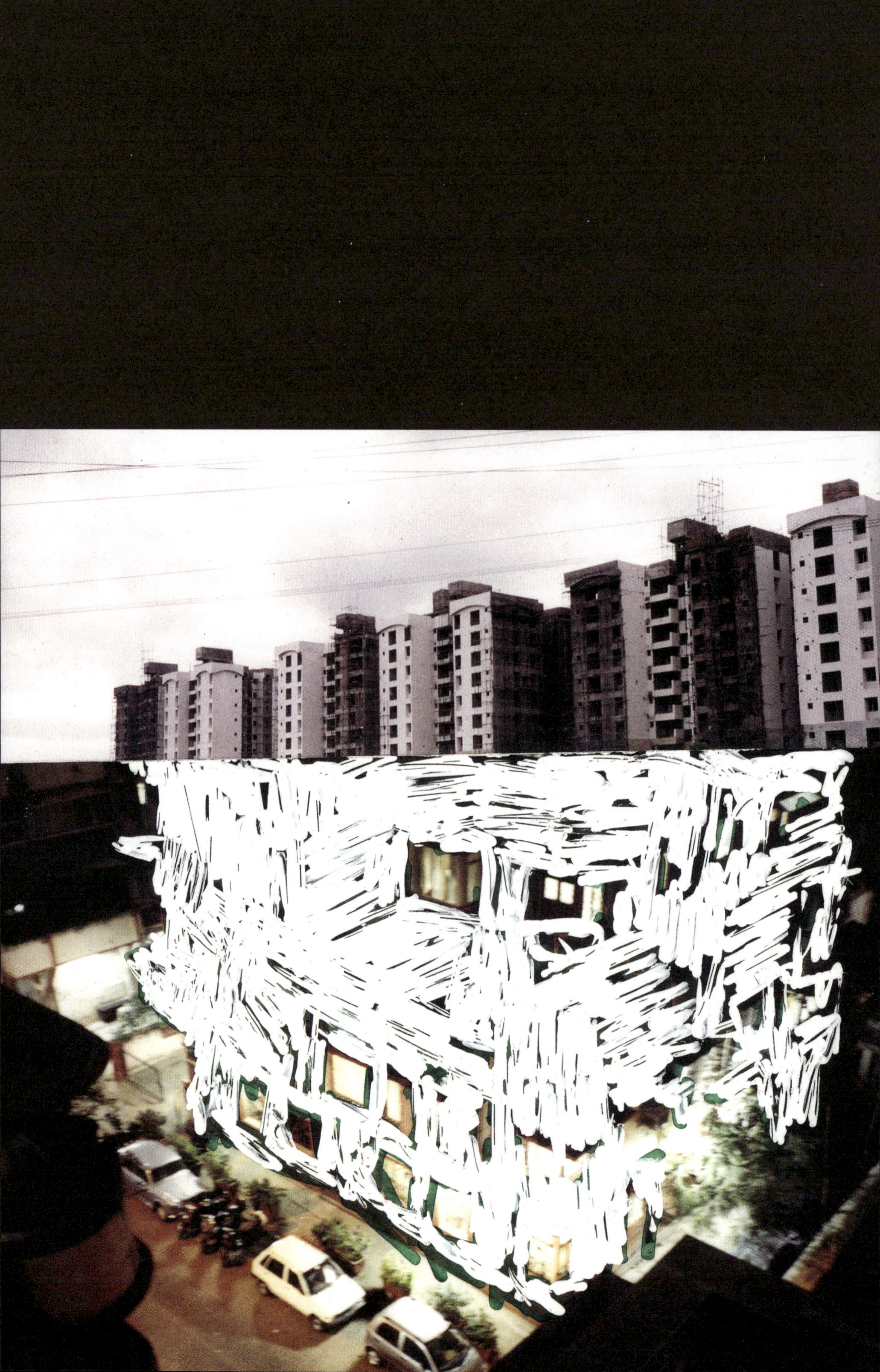

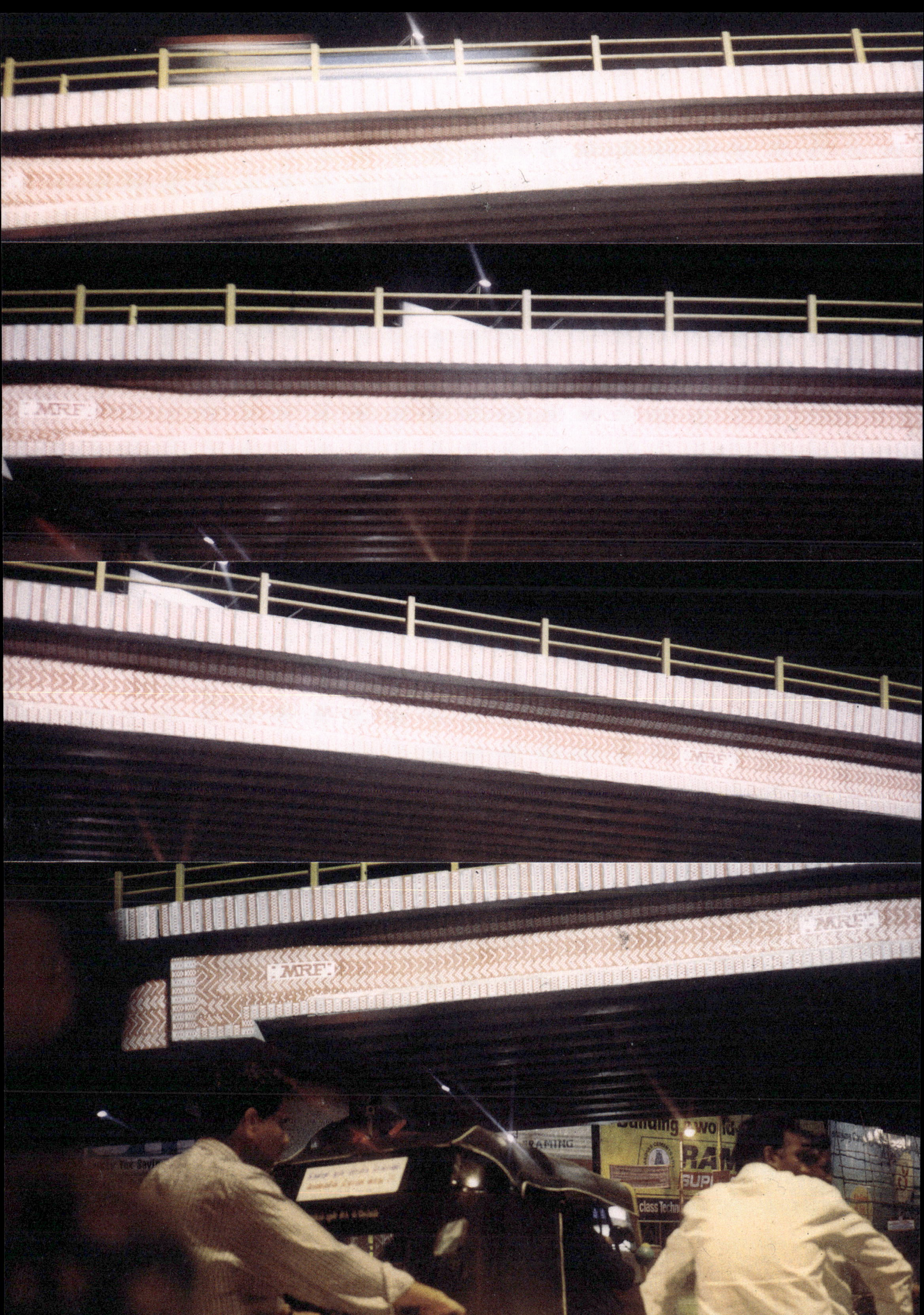
MRF
MRF
MRF
MRF

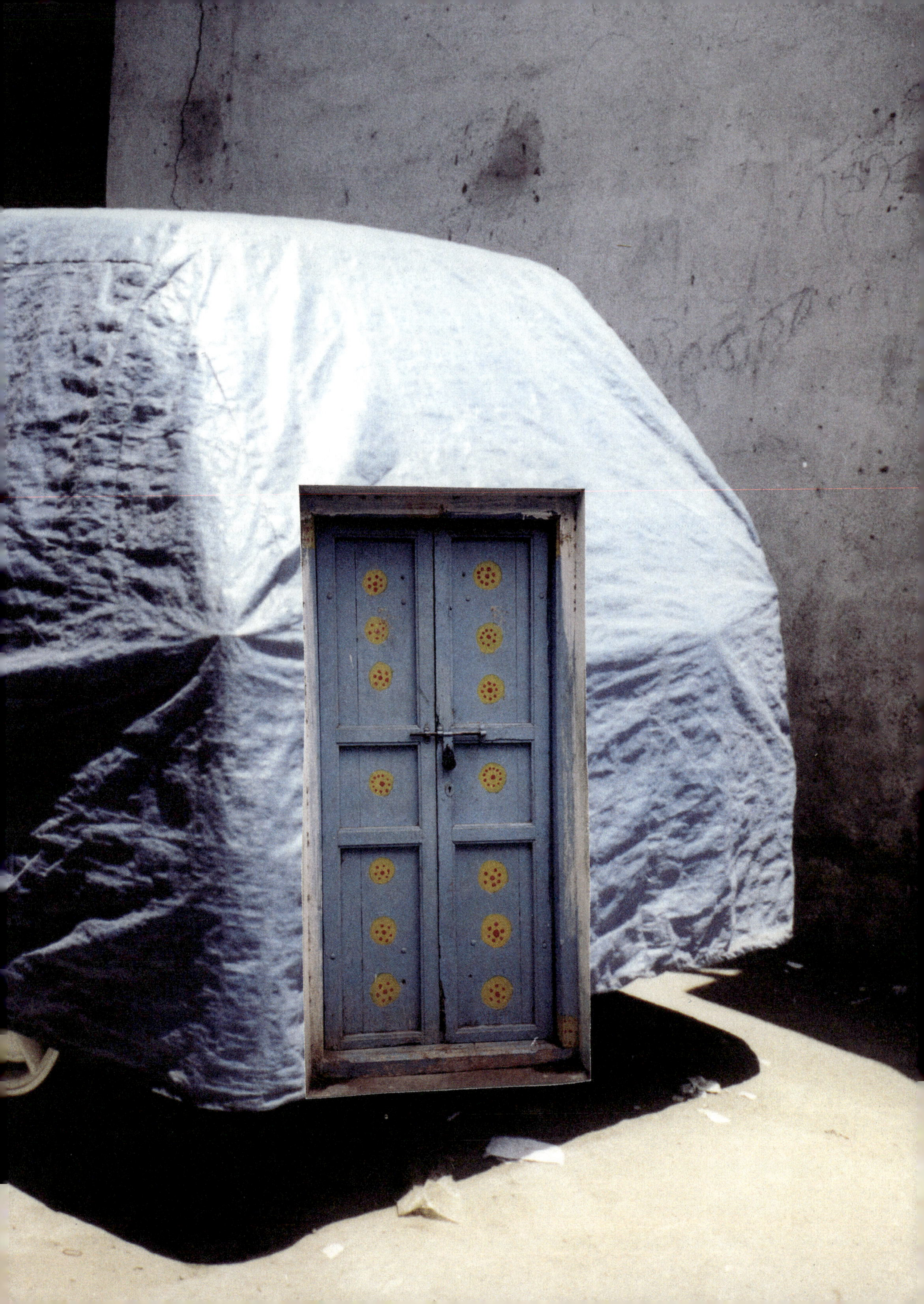

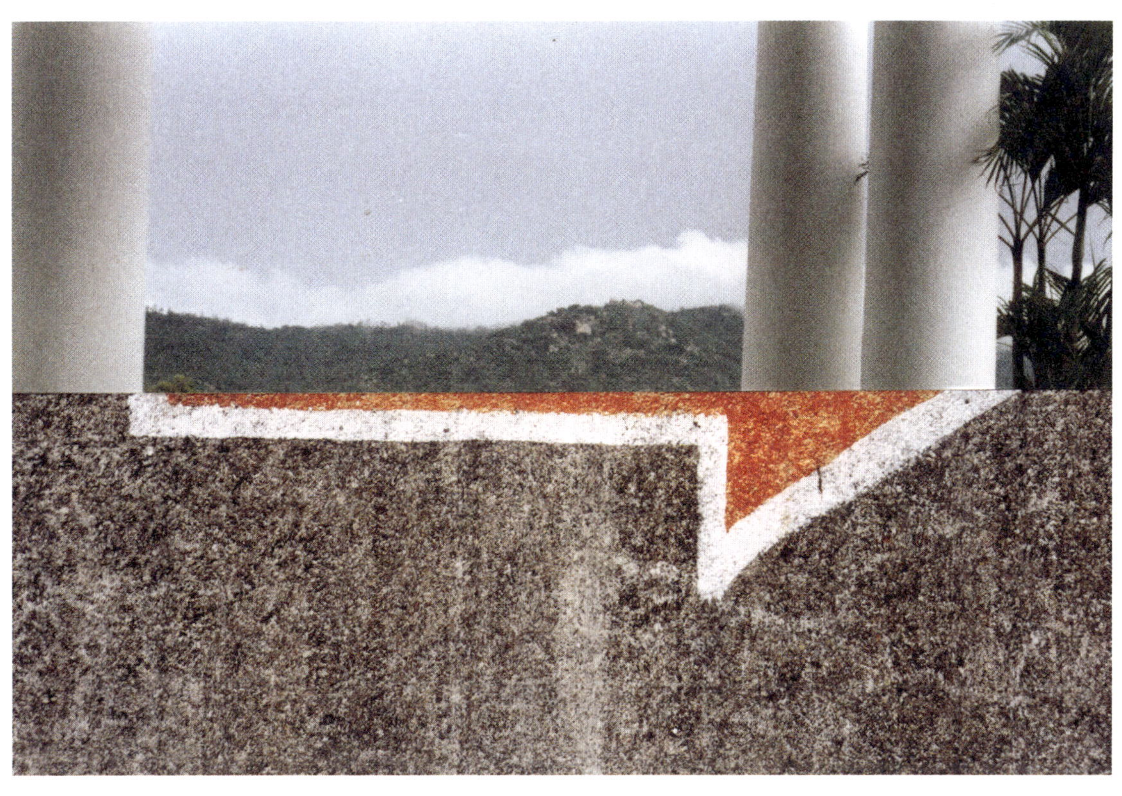

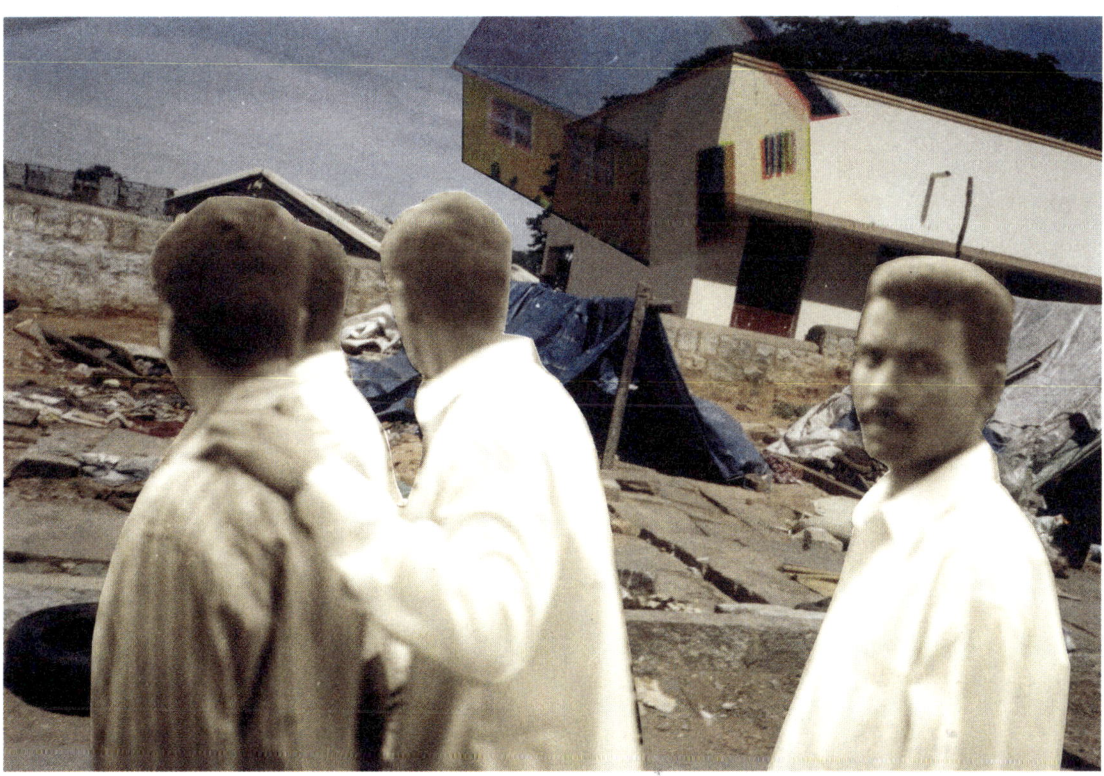

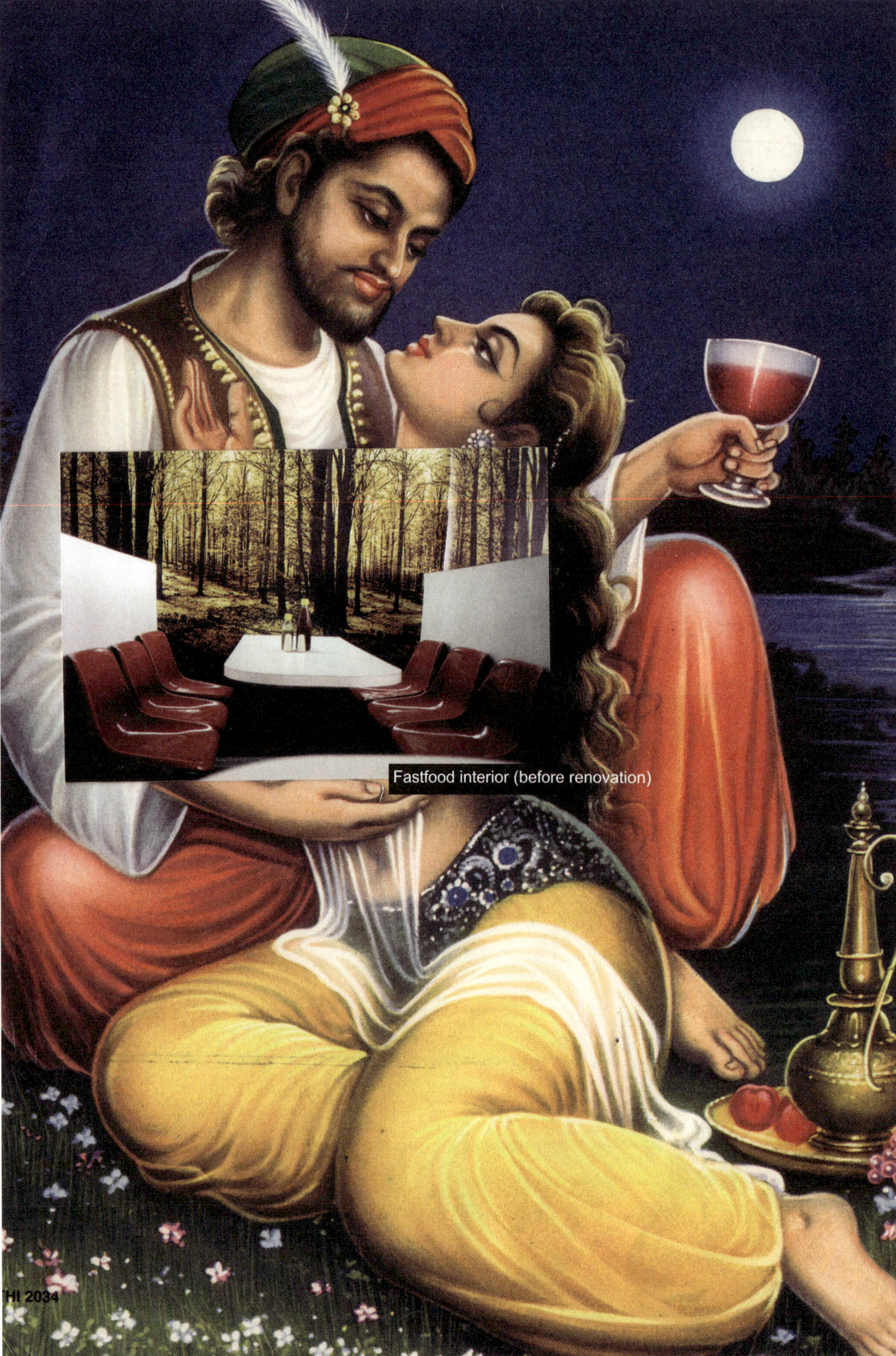
Fastfood interior (before renovation)
THI 2034

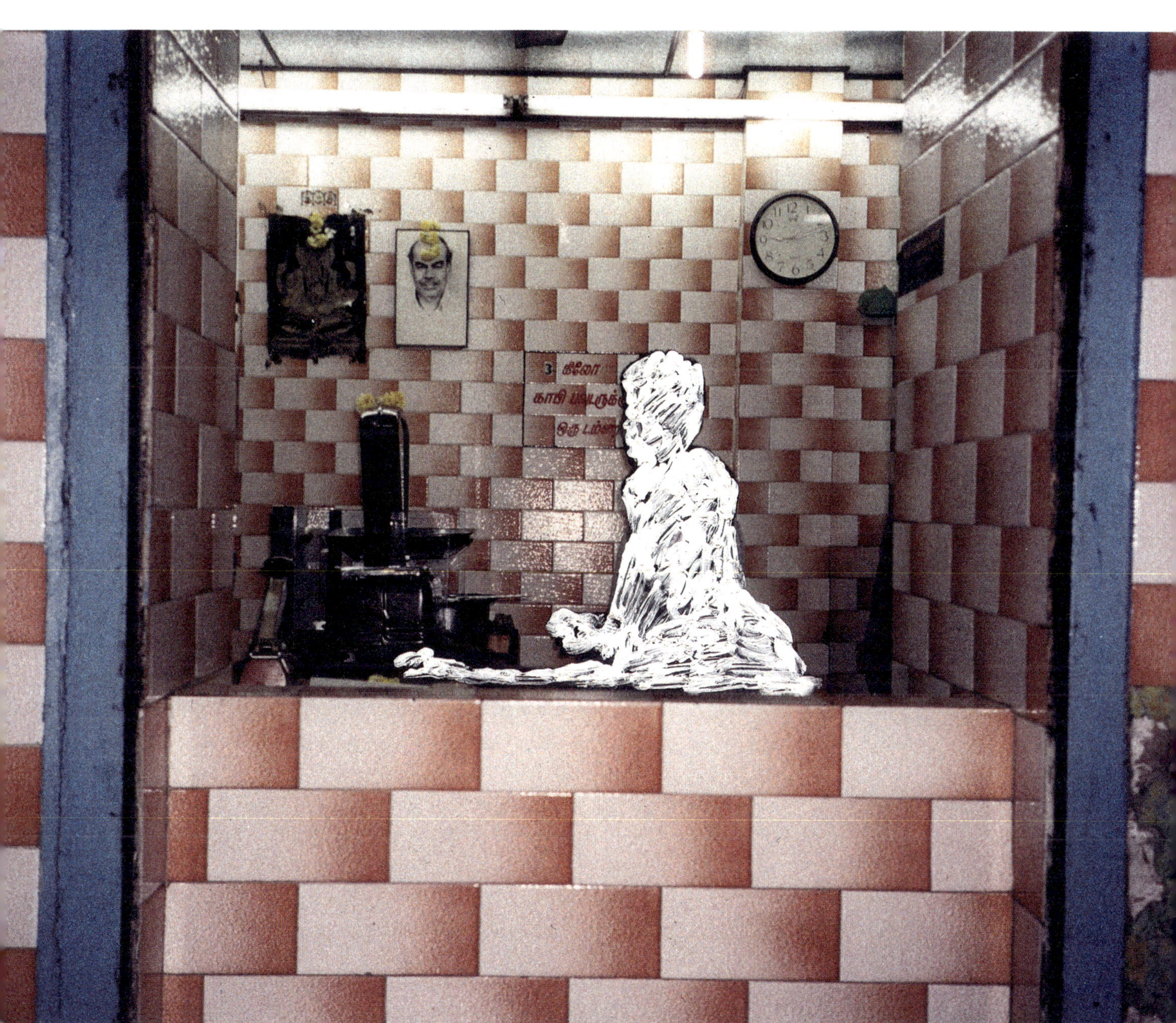
3 கிலோ
காபி
ஒரு

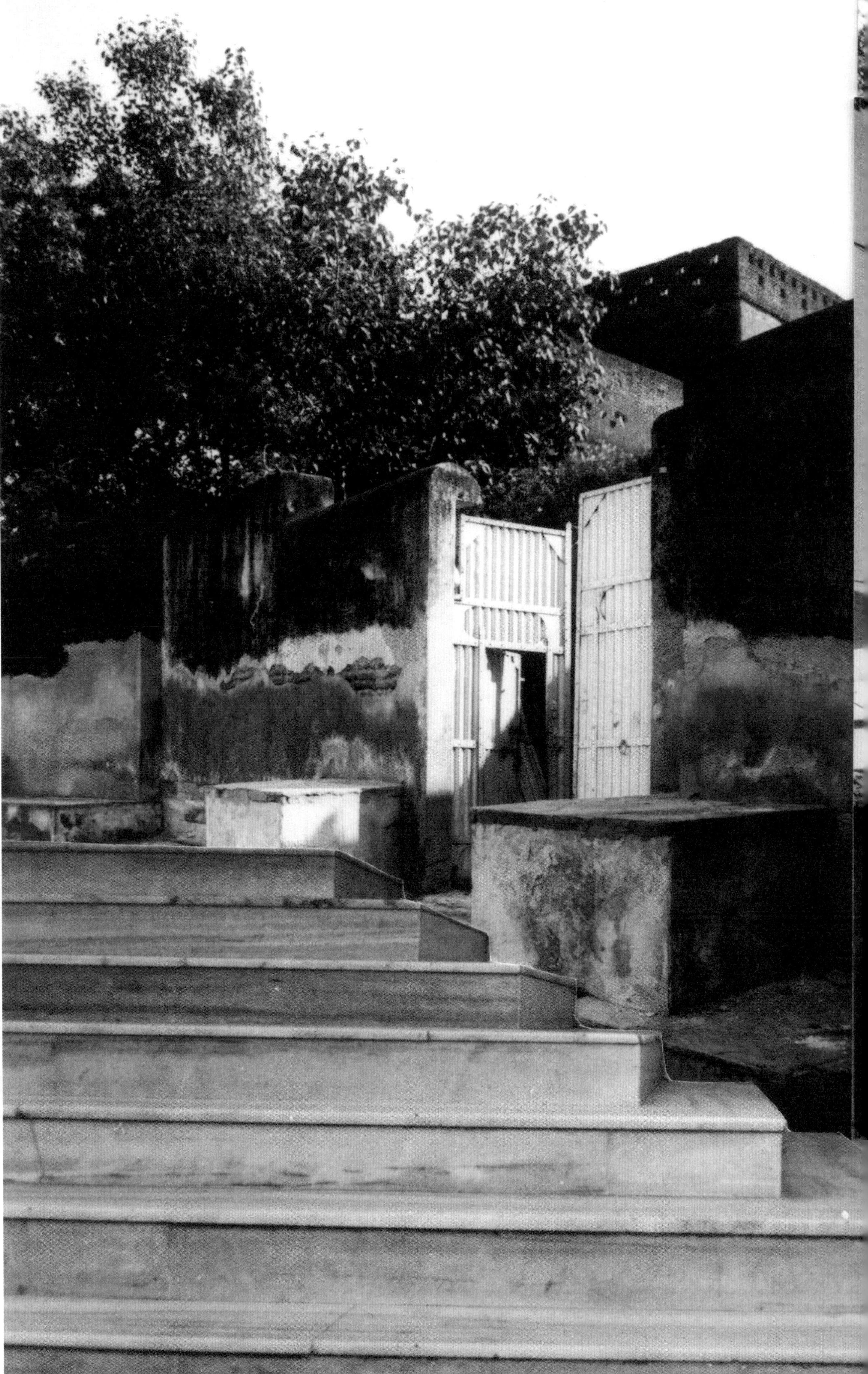

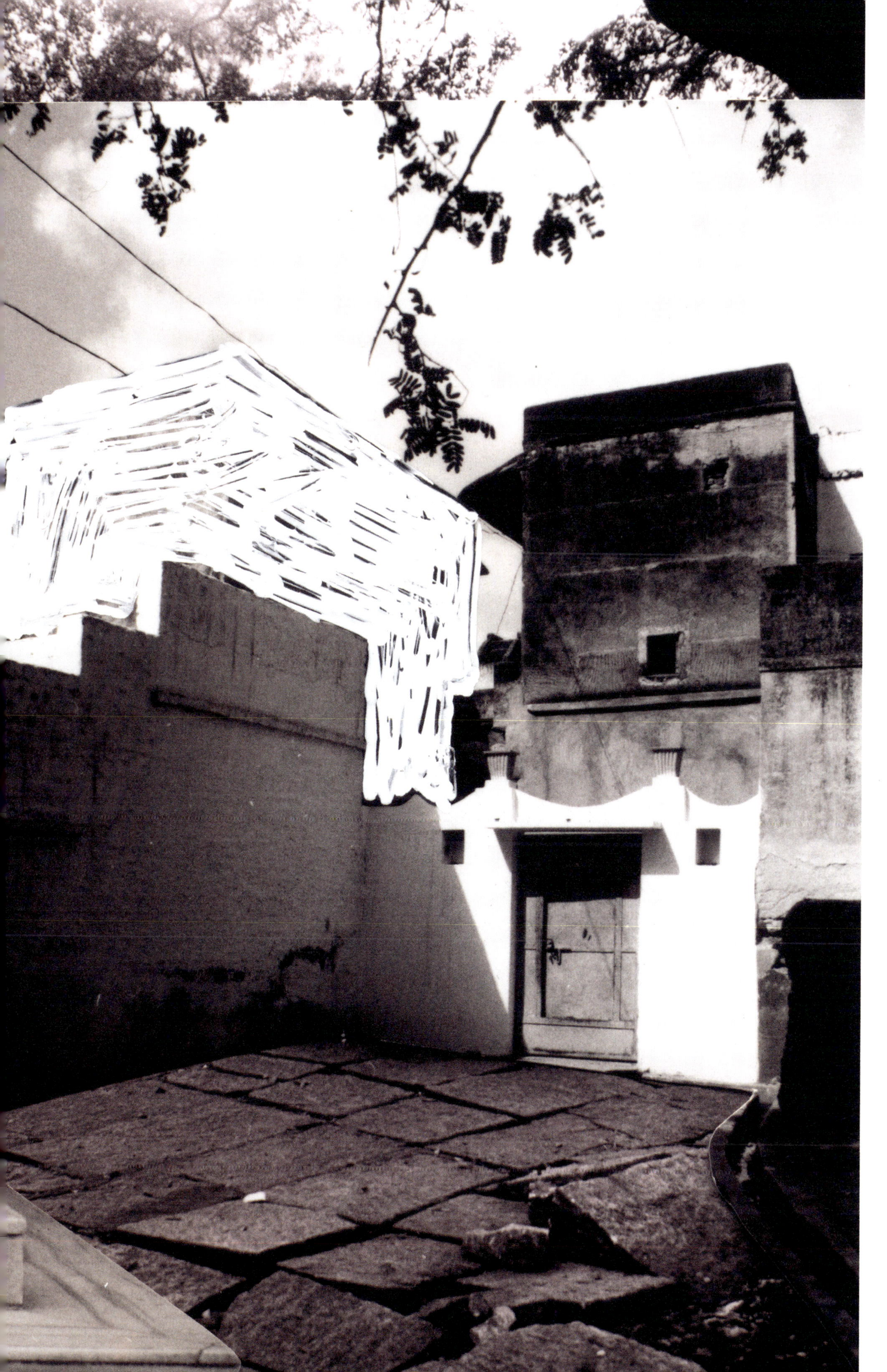

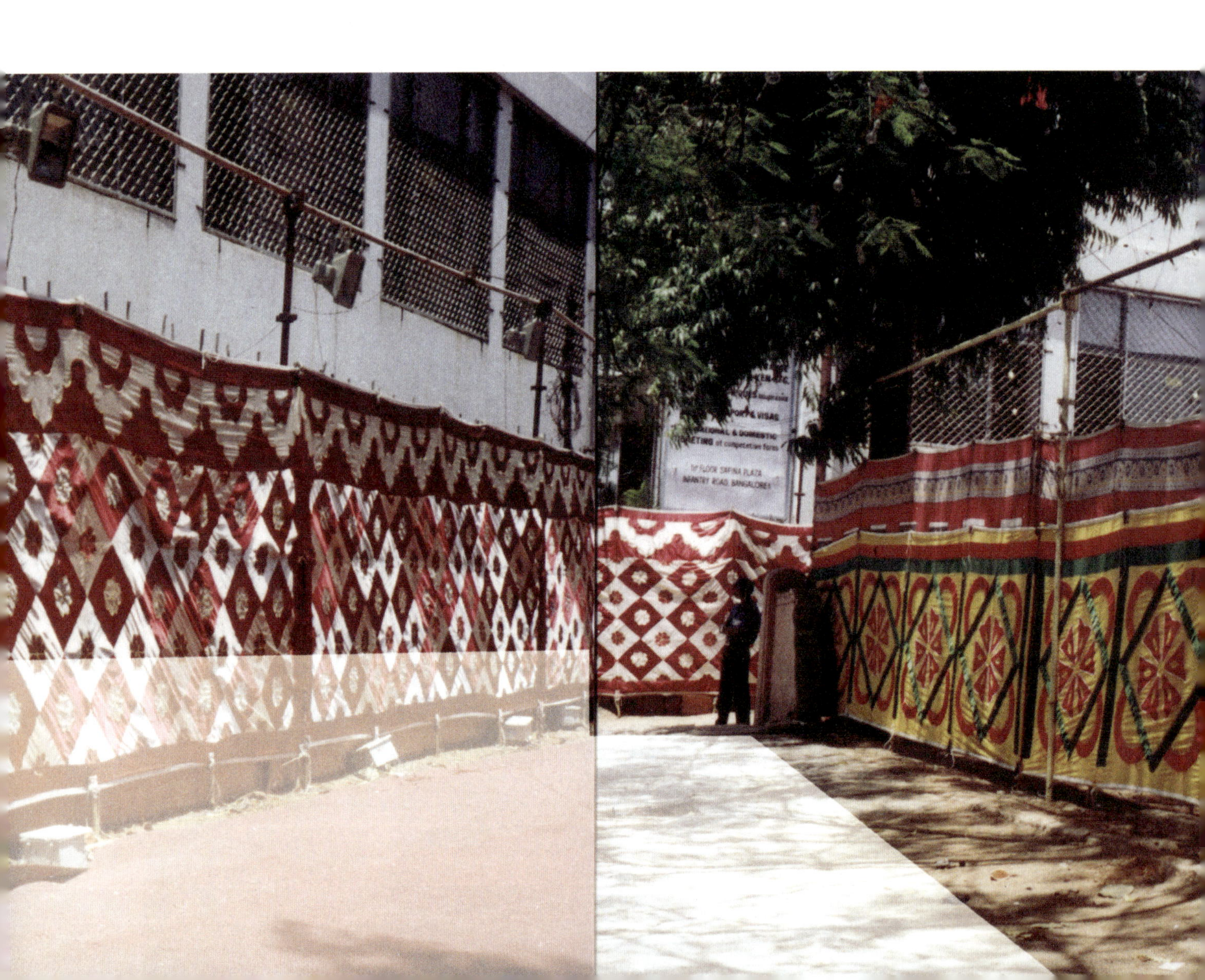

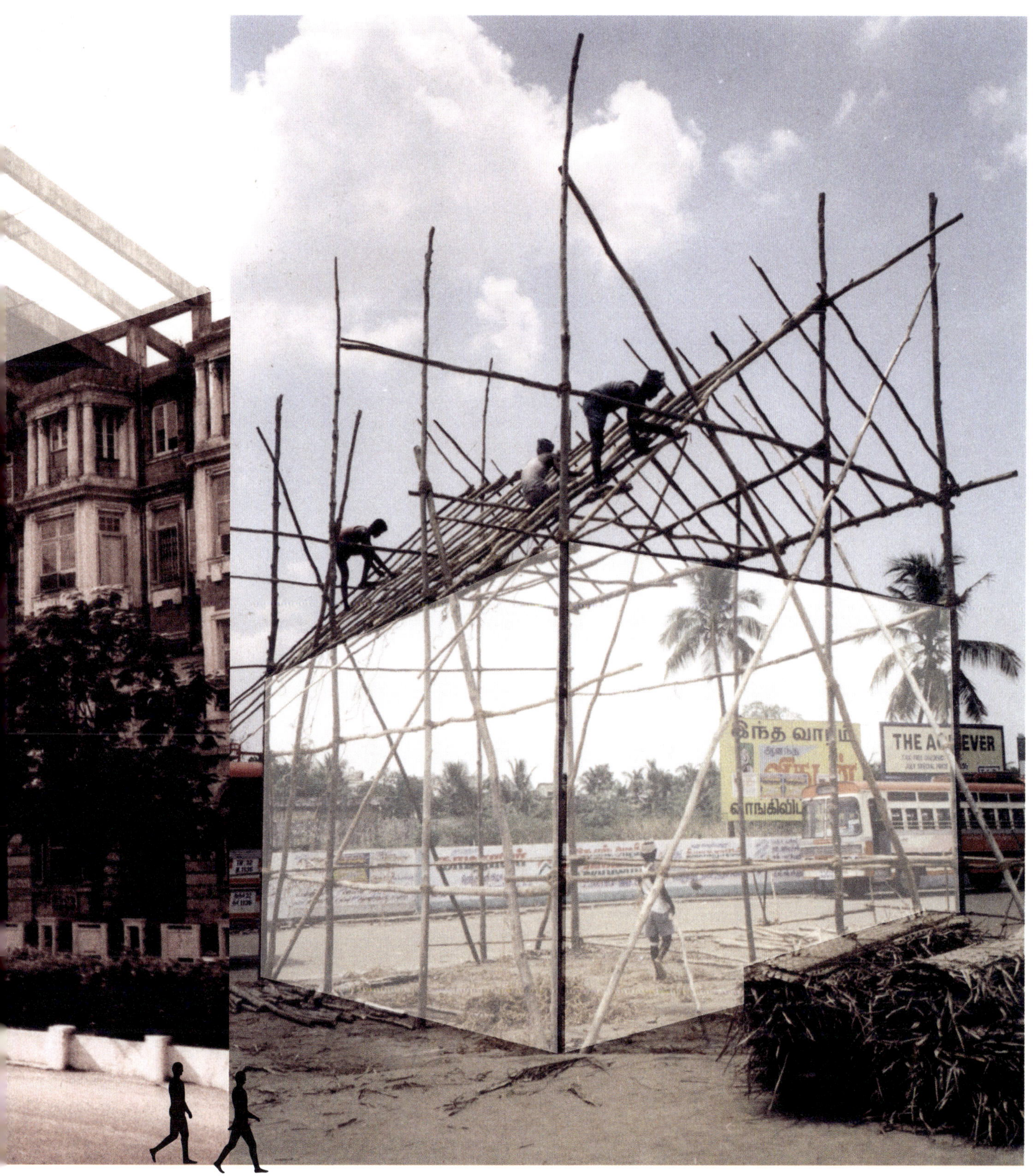

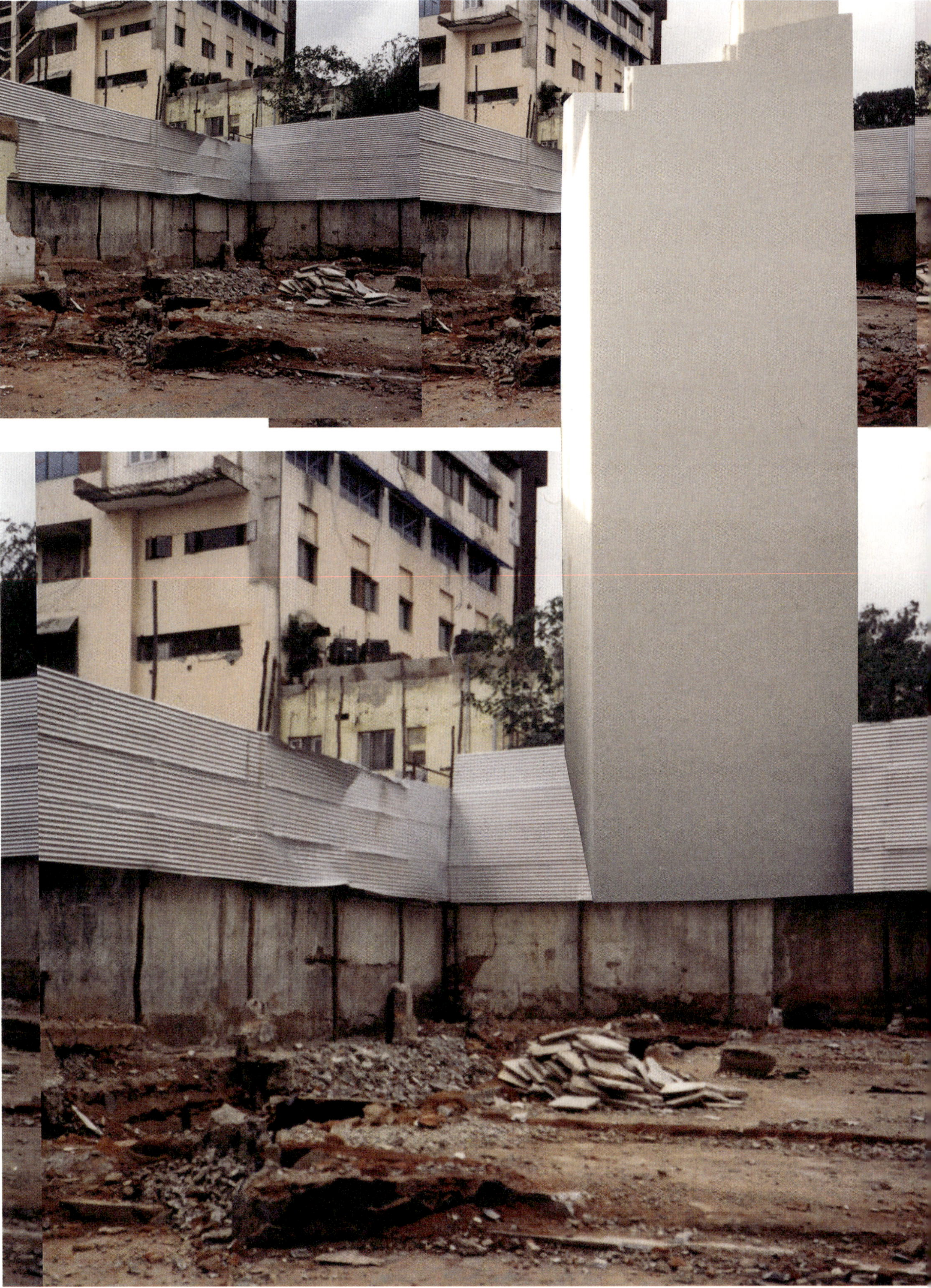

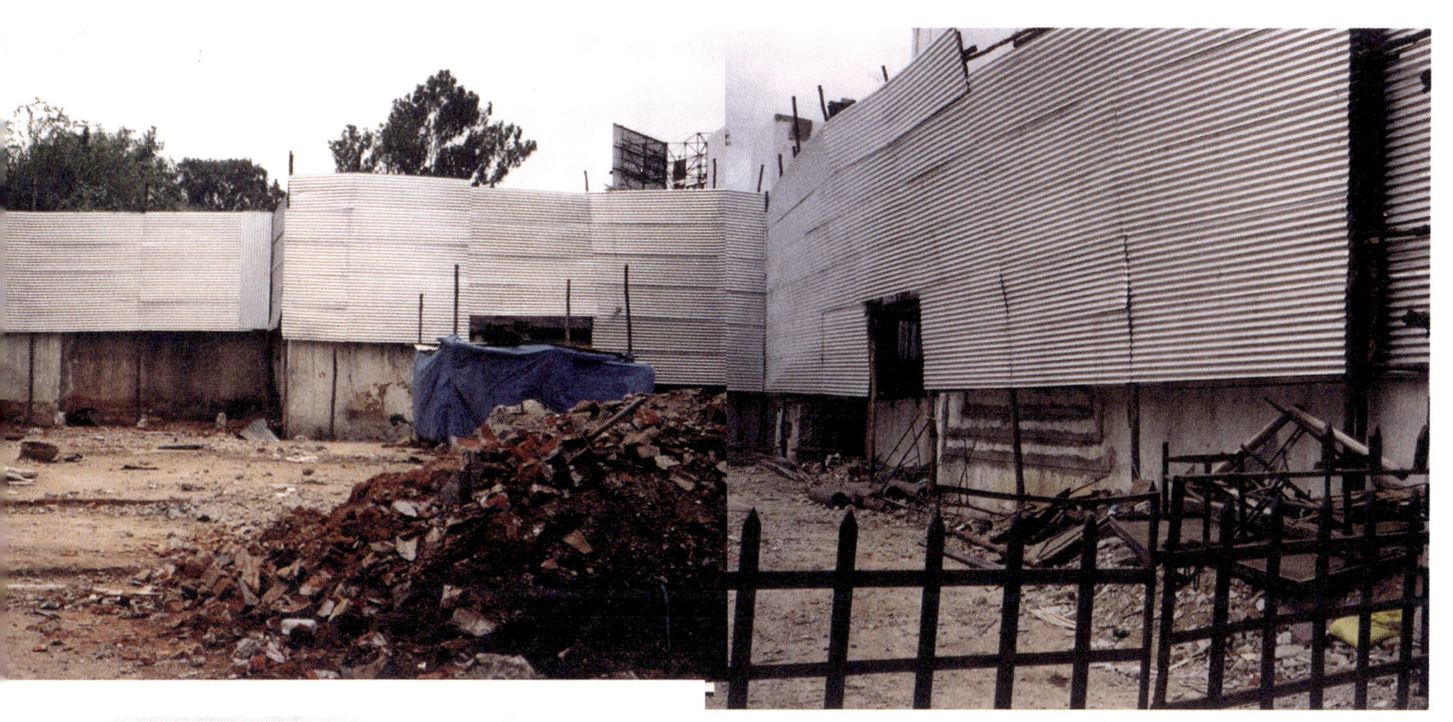

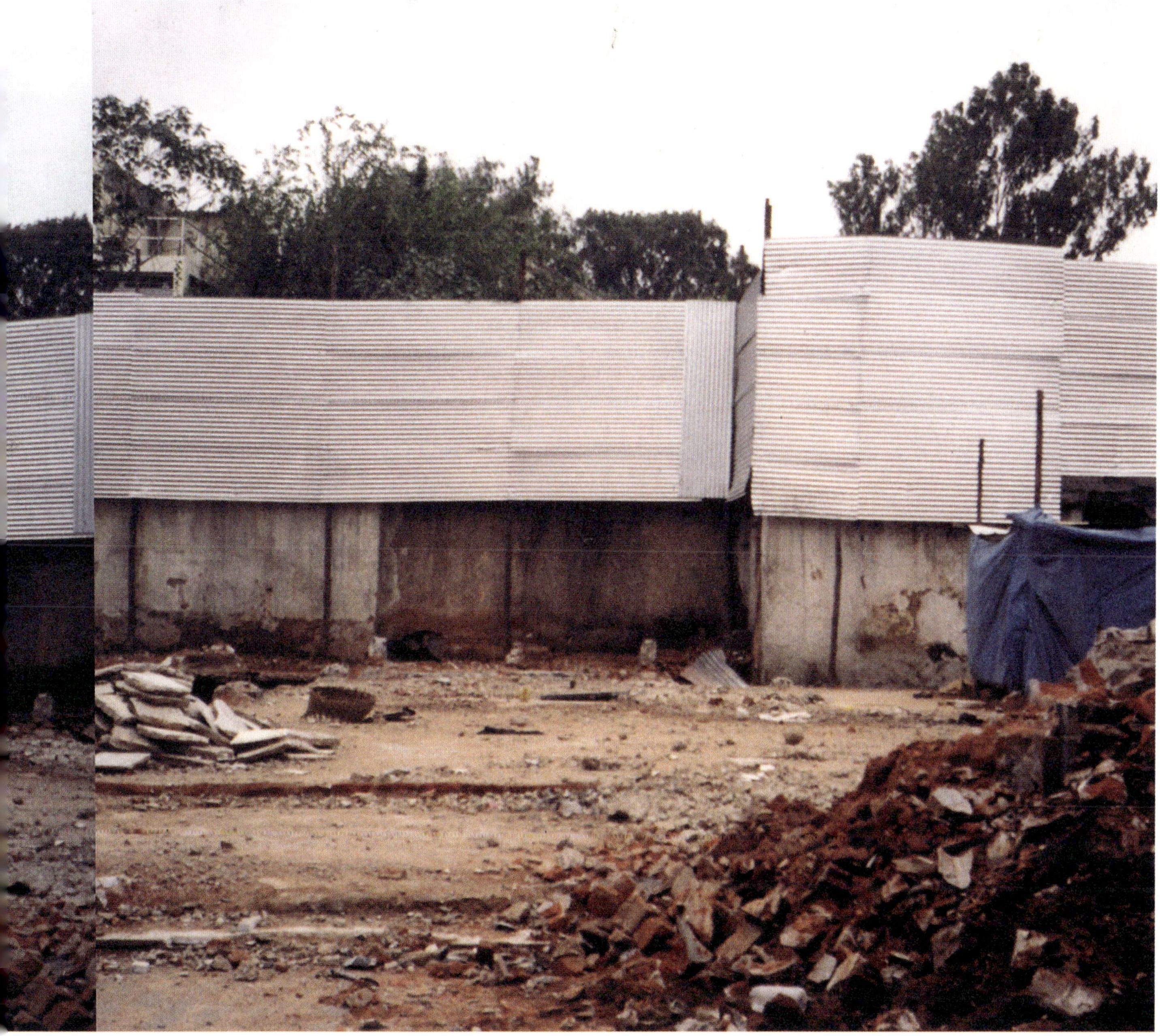

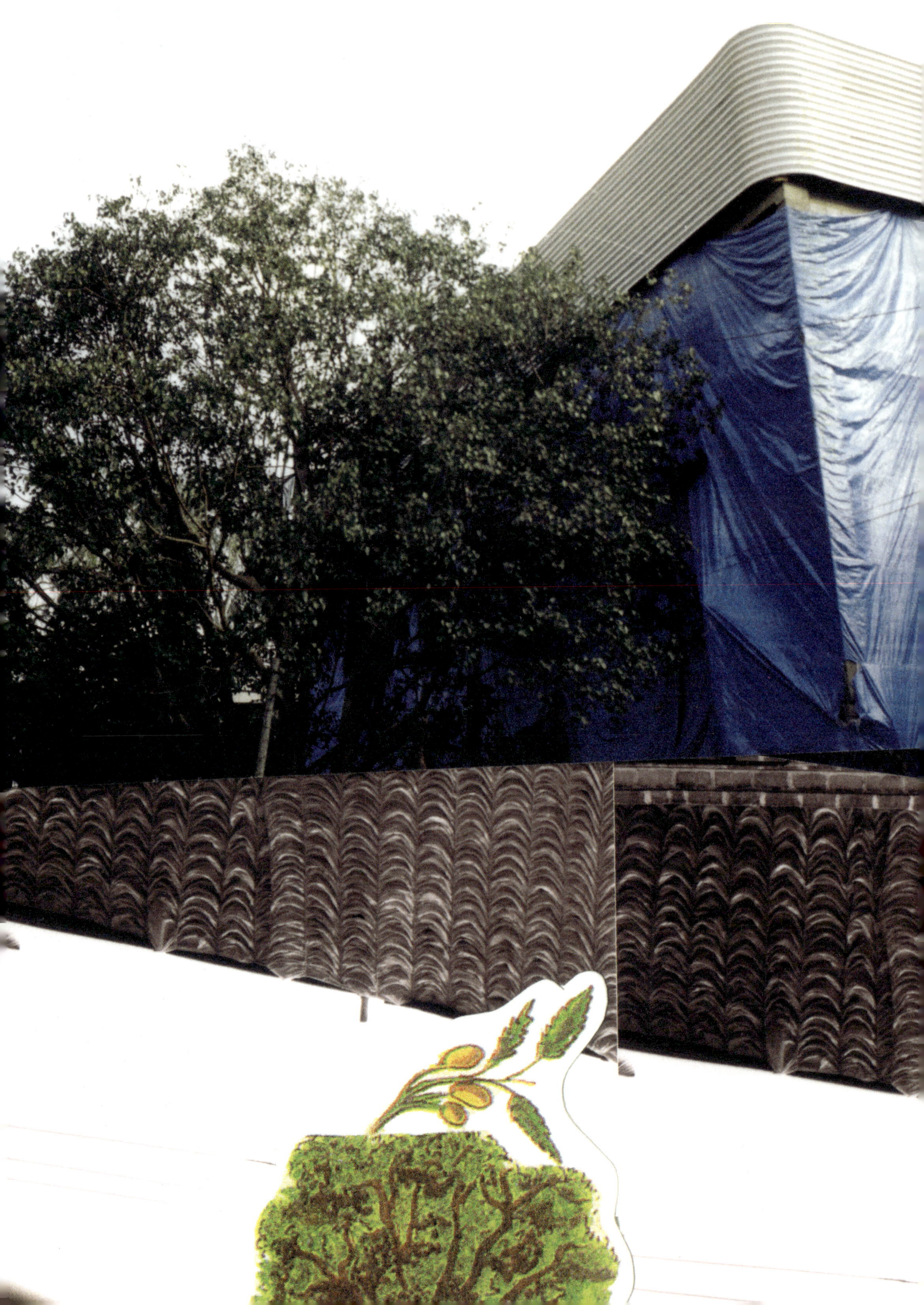

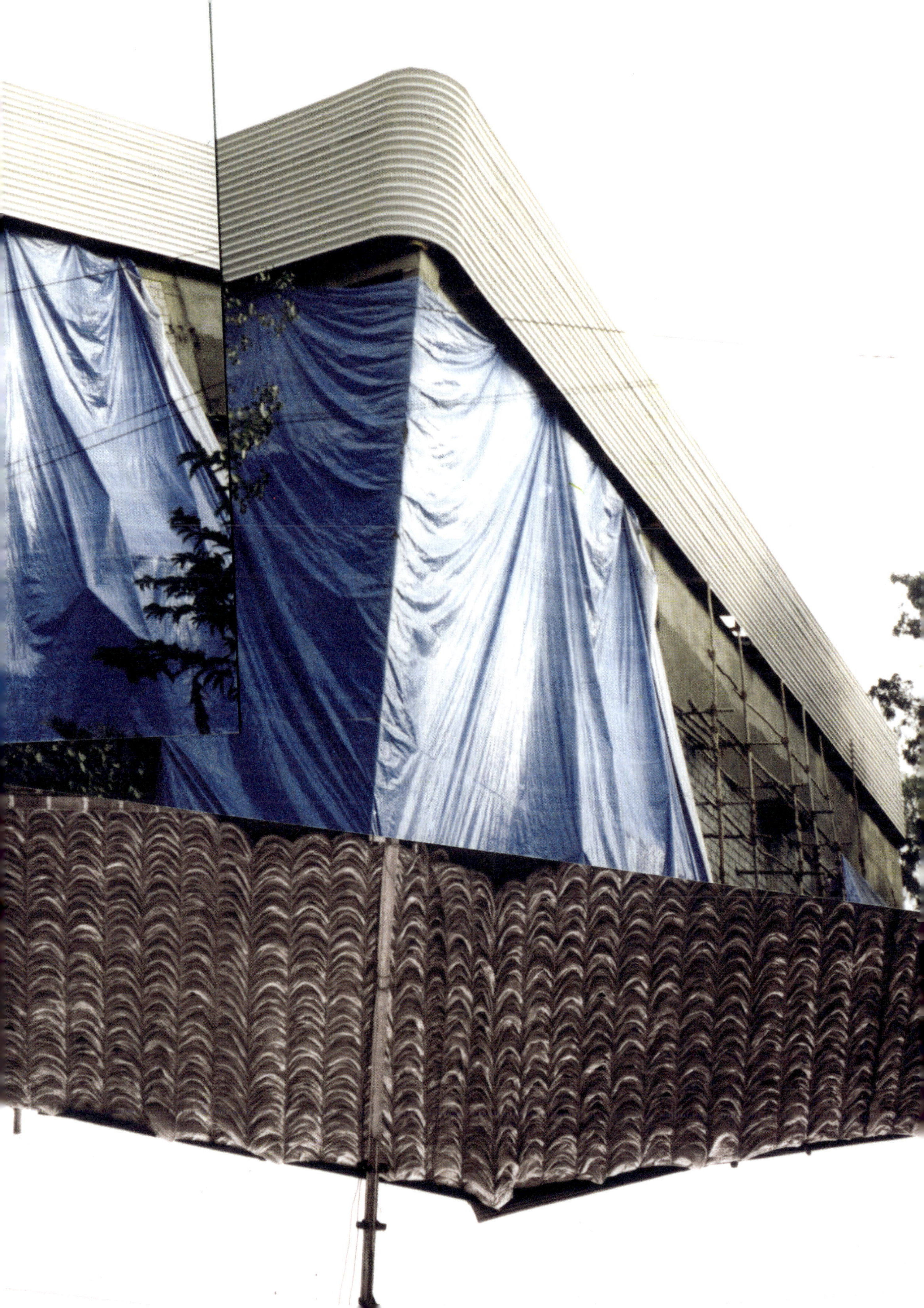

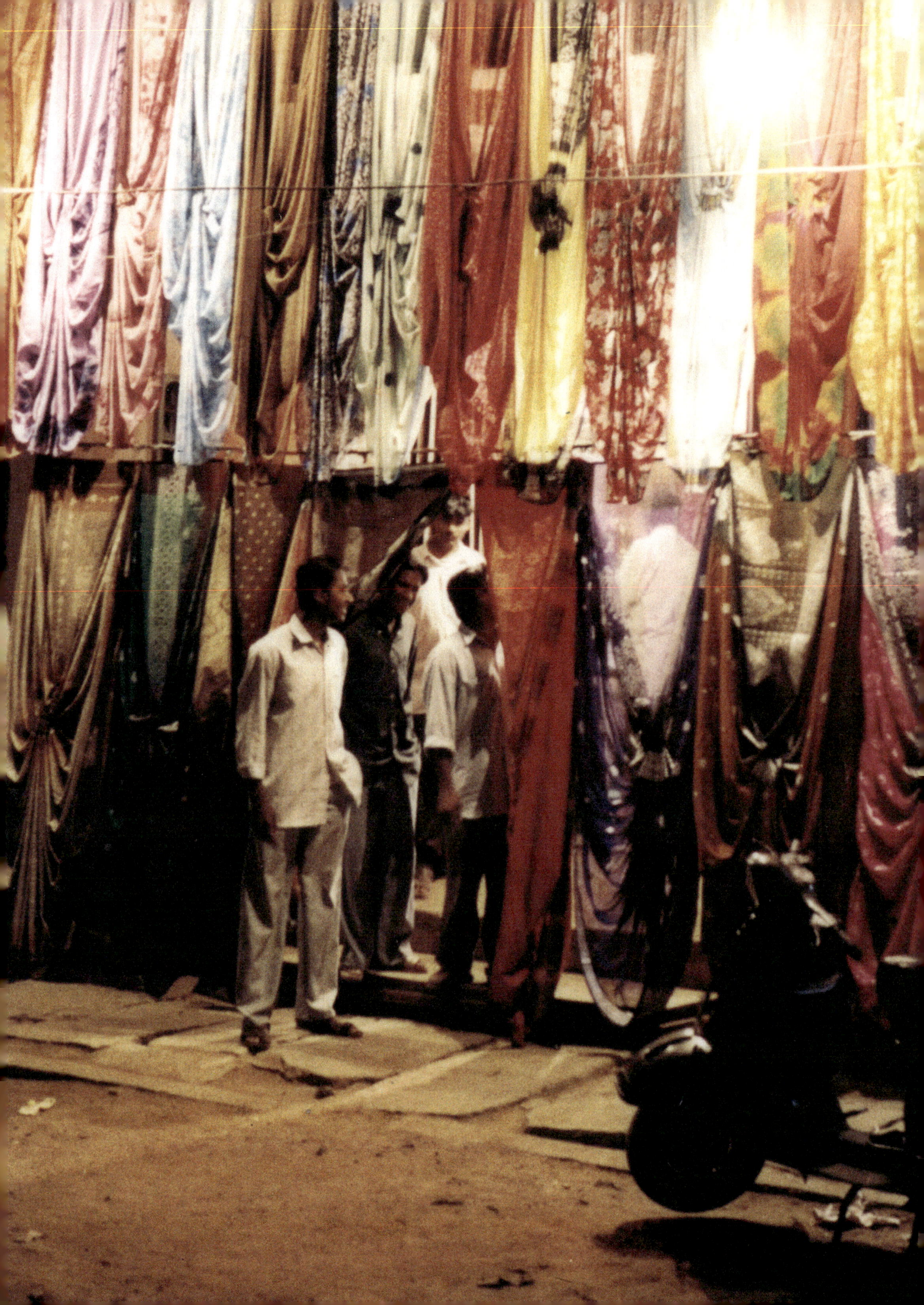

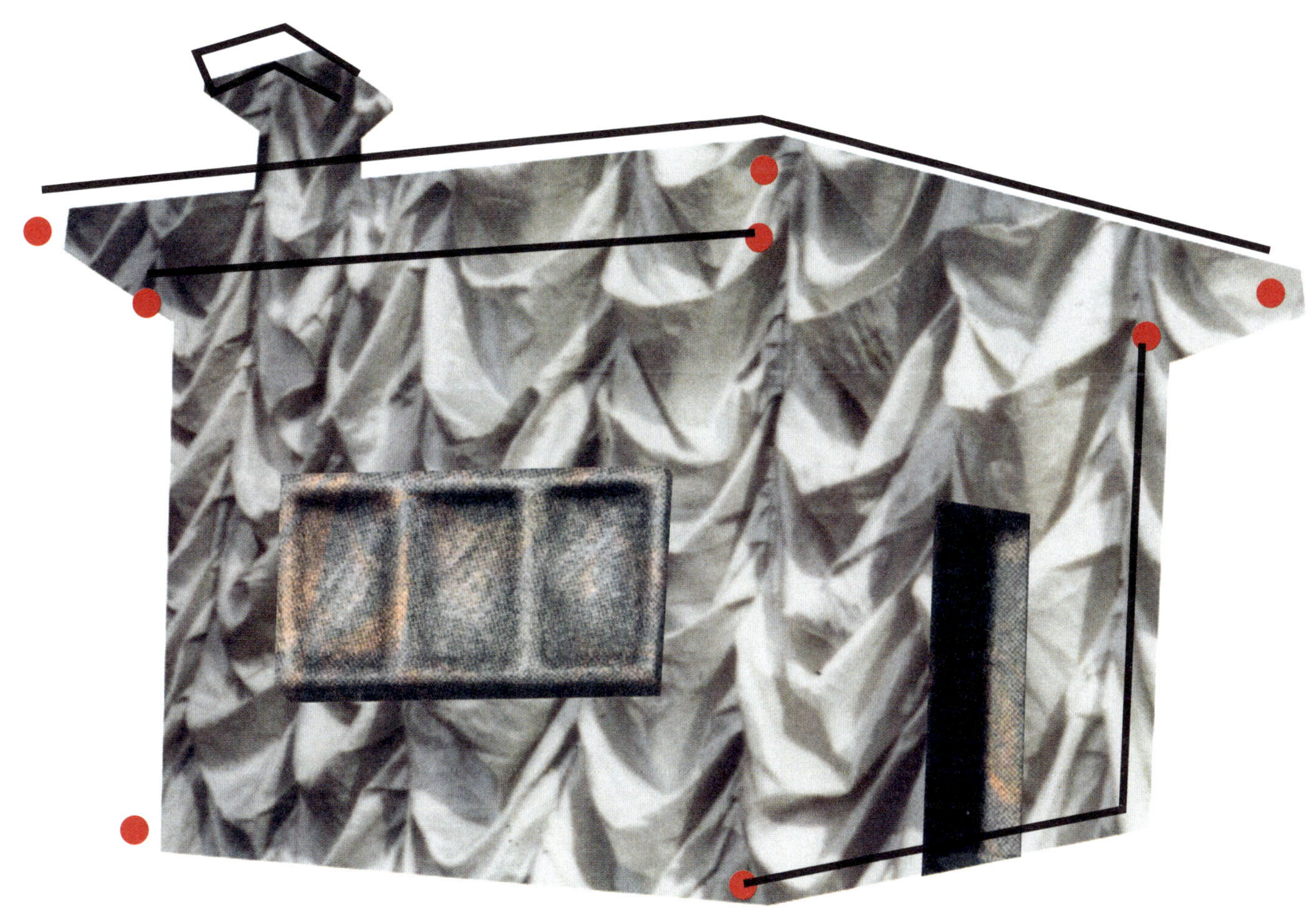

connect the dots

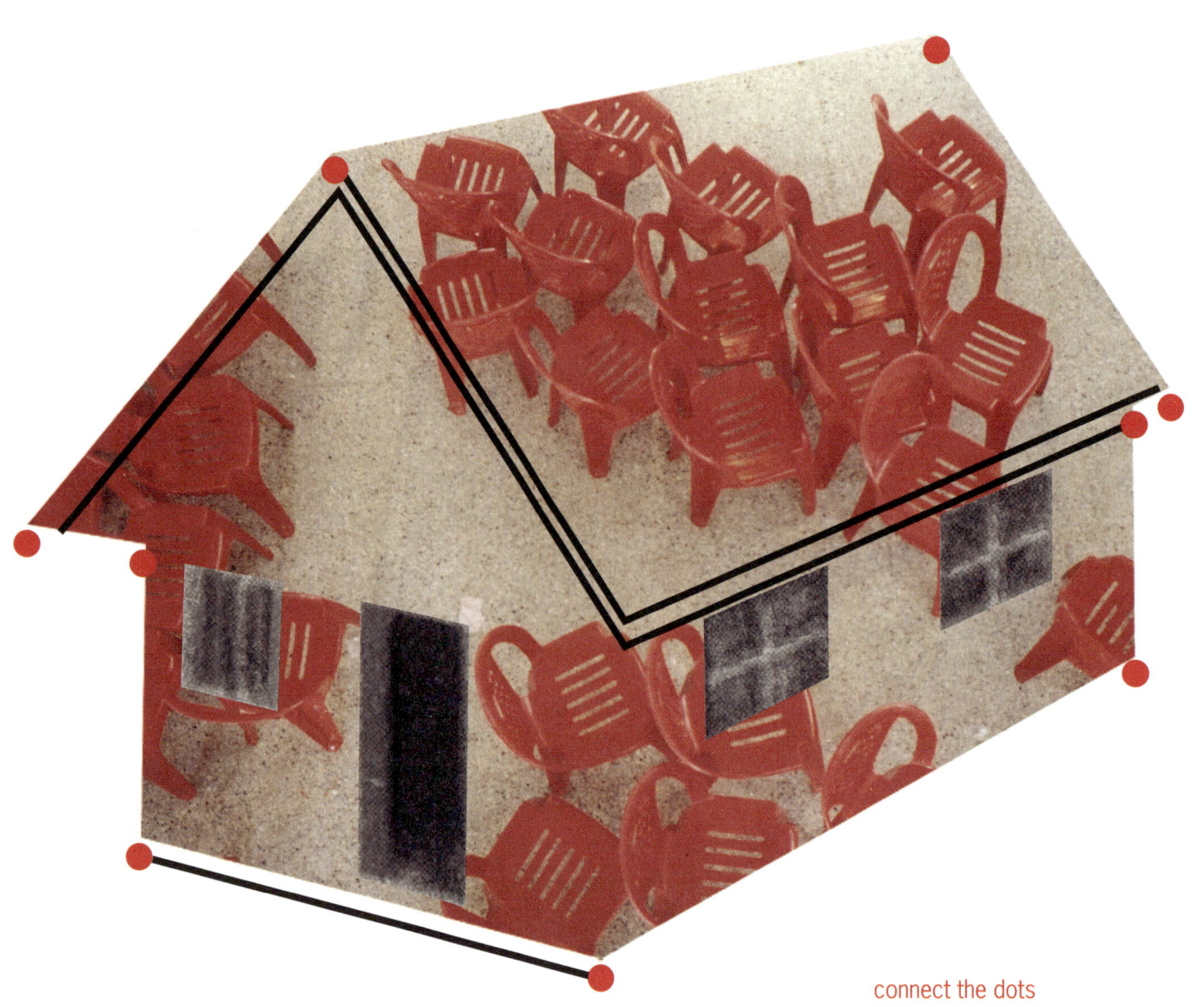

connect the dots

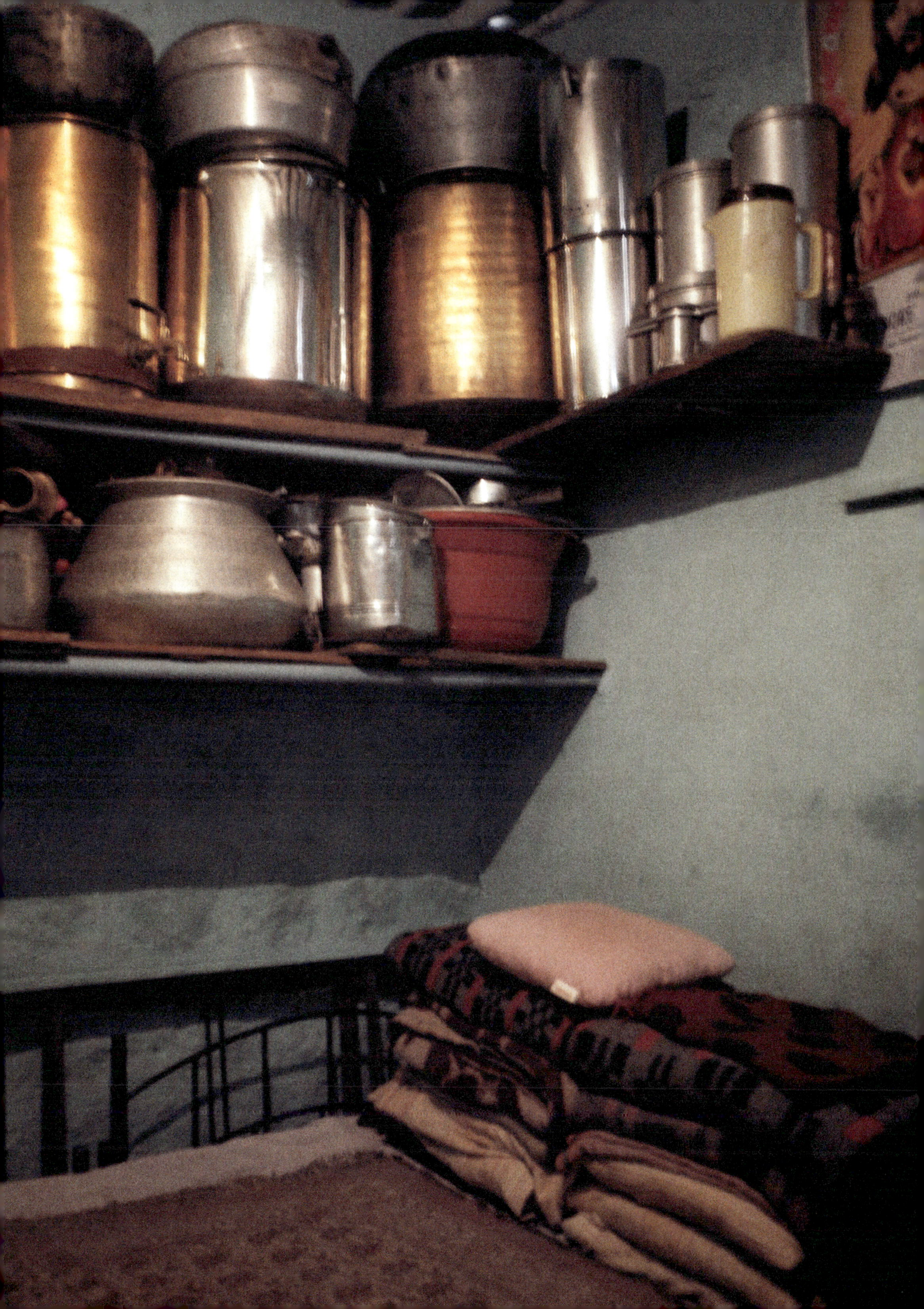

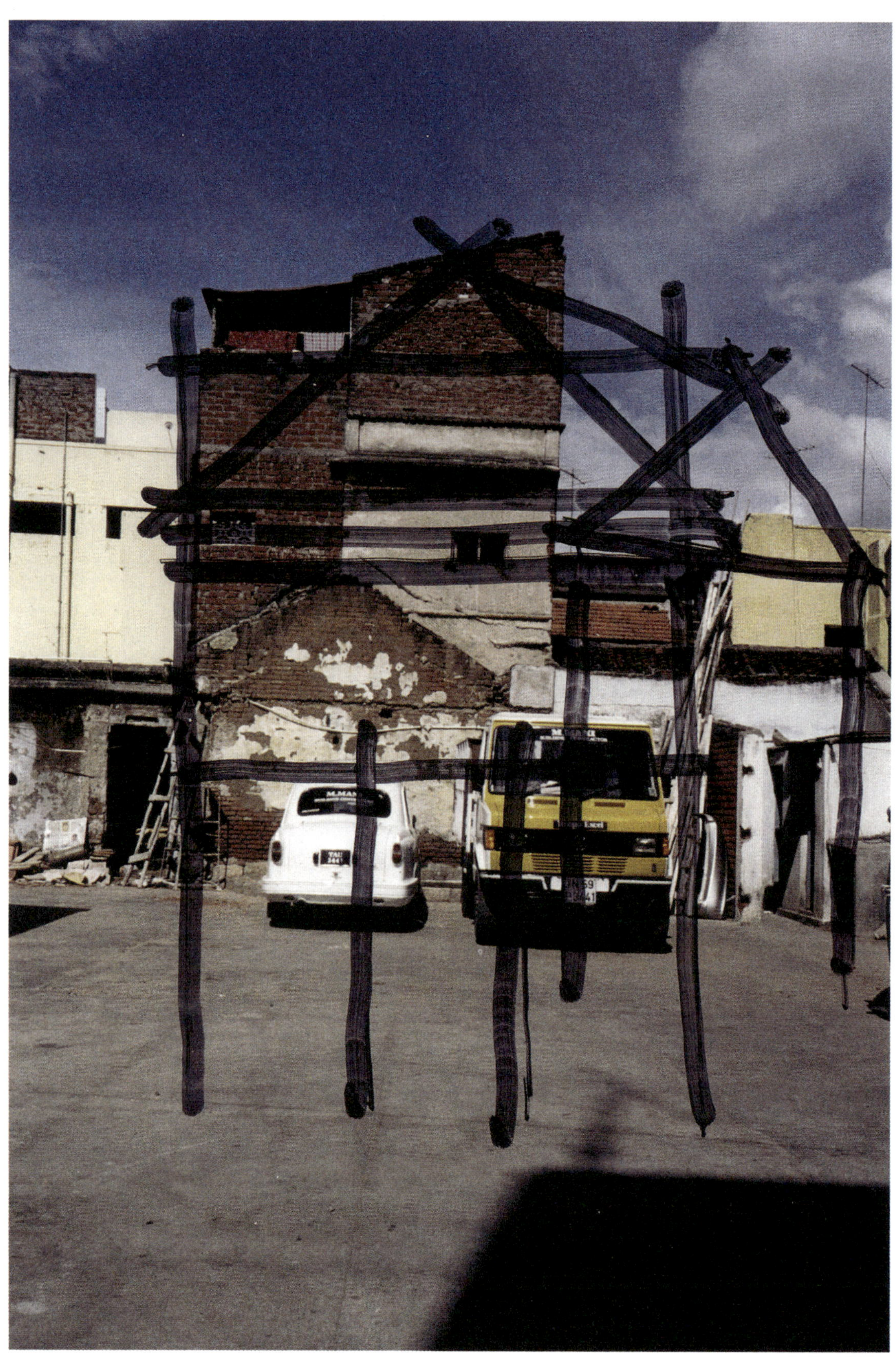

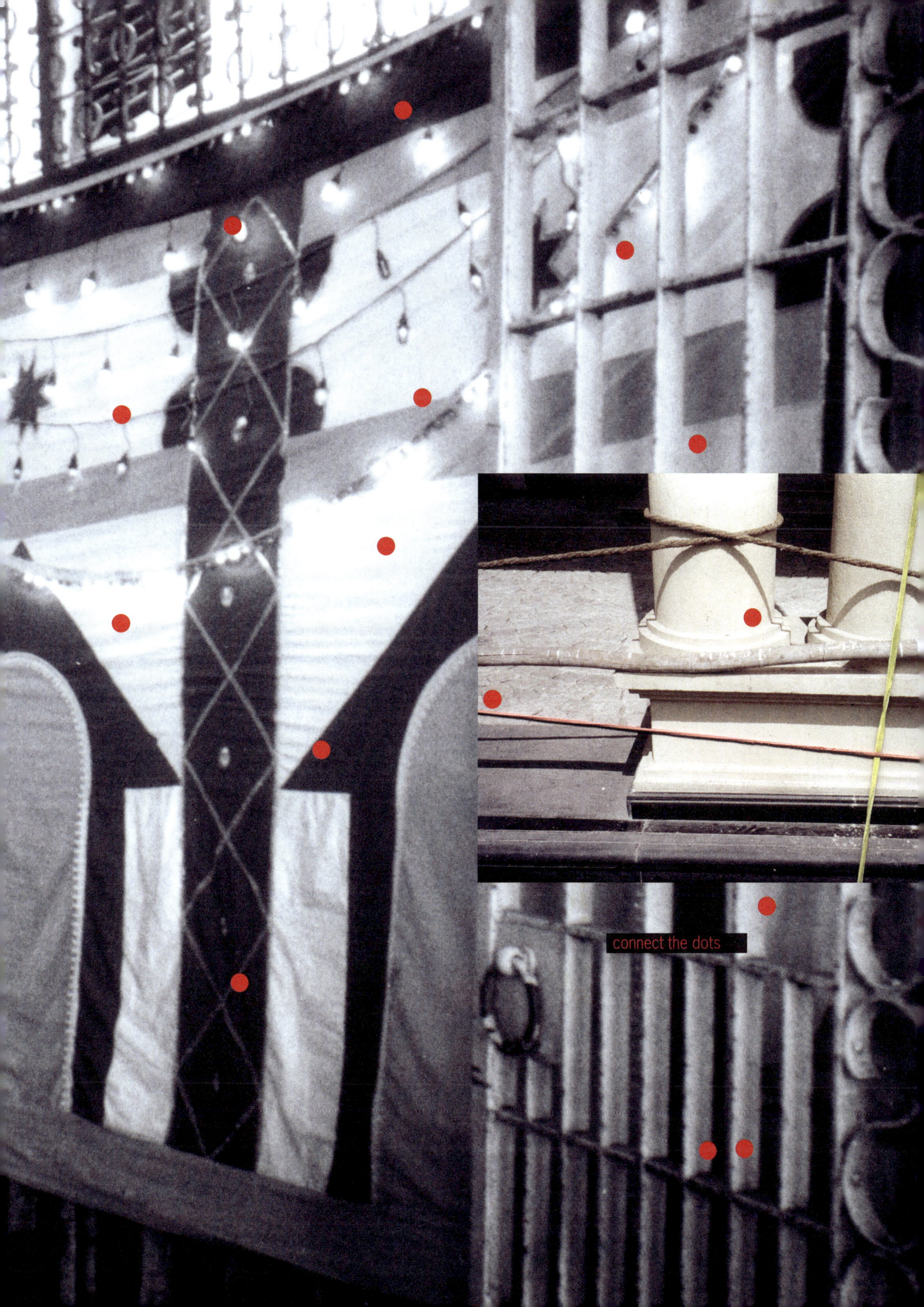
connect the dots

Remote City

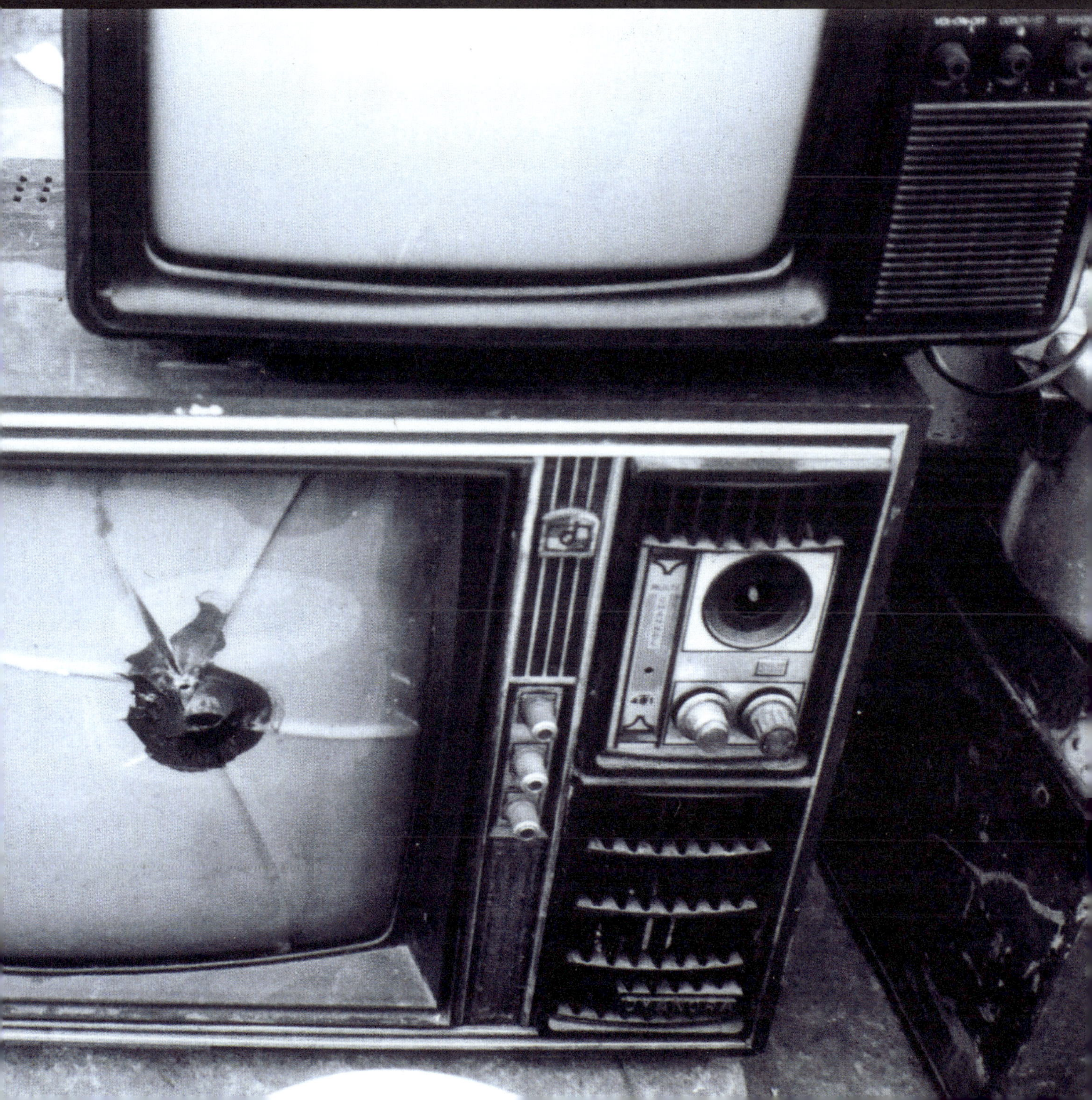

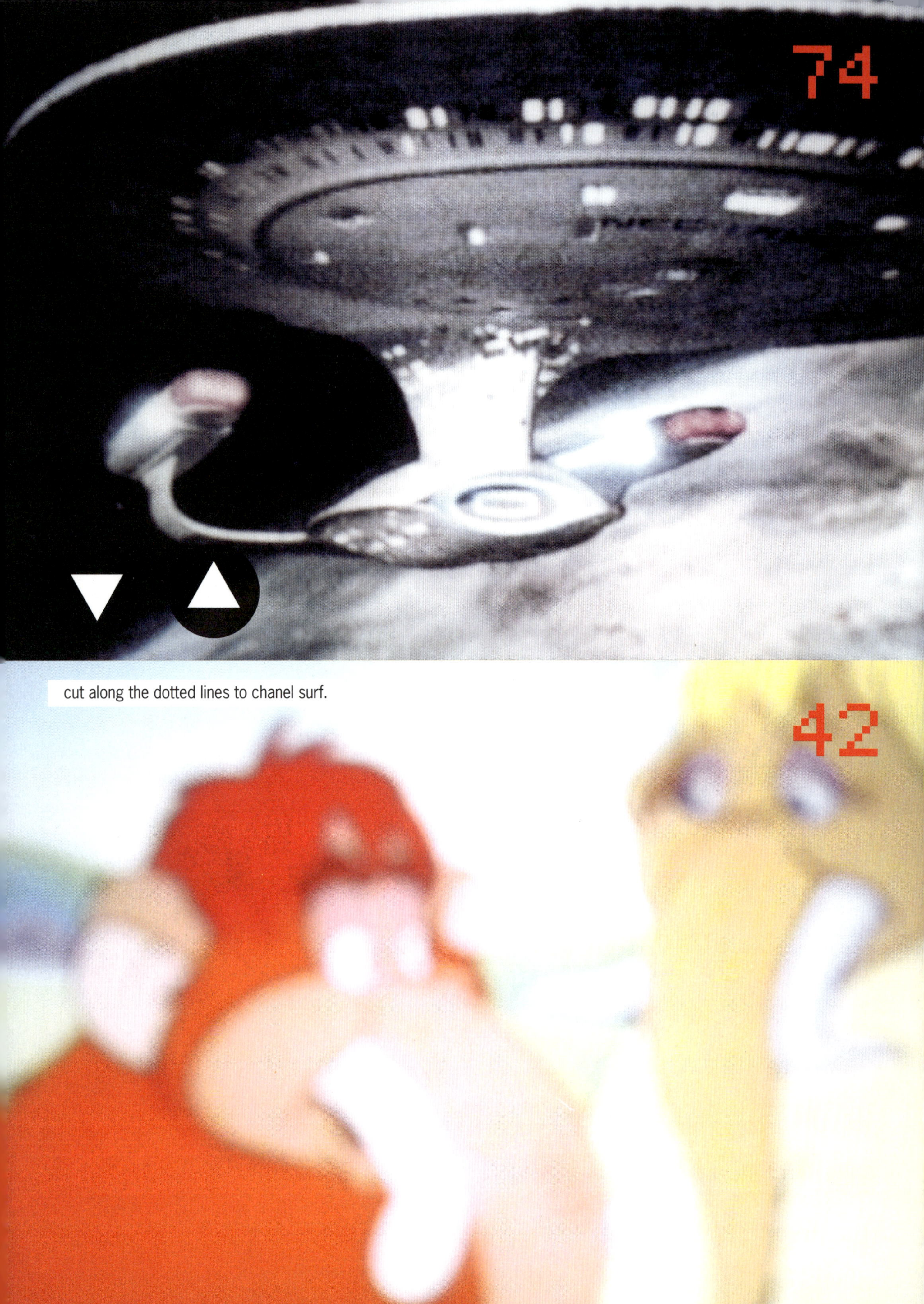
74
cut along the dotted lines to chanel surf.
42

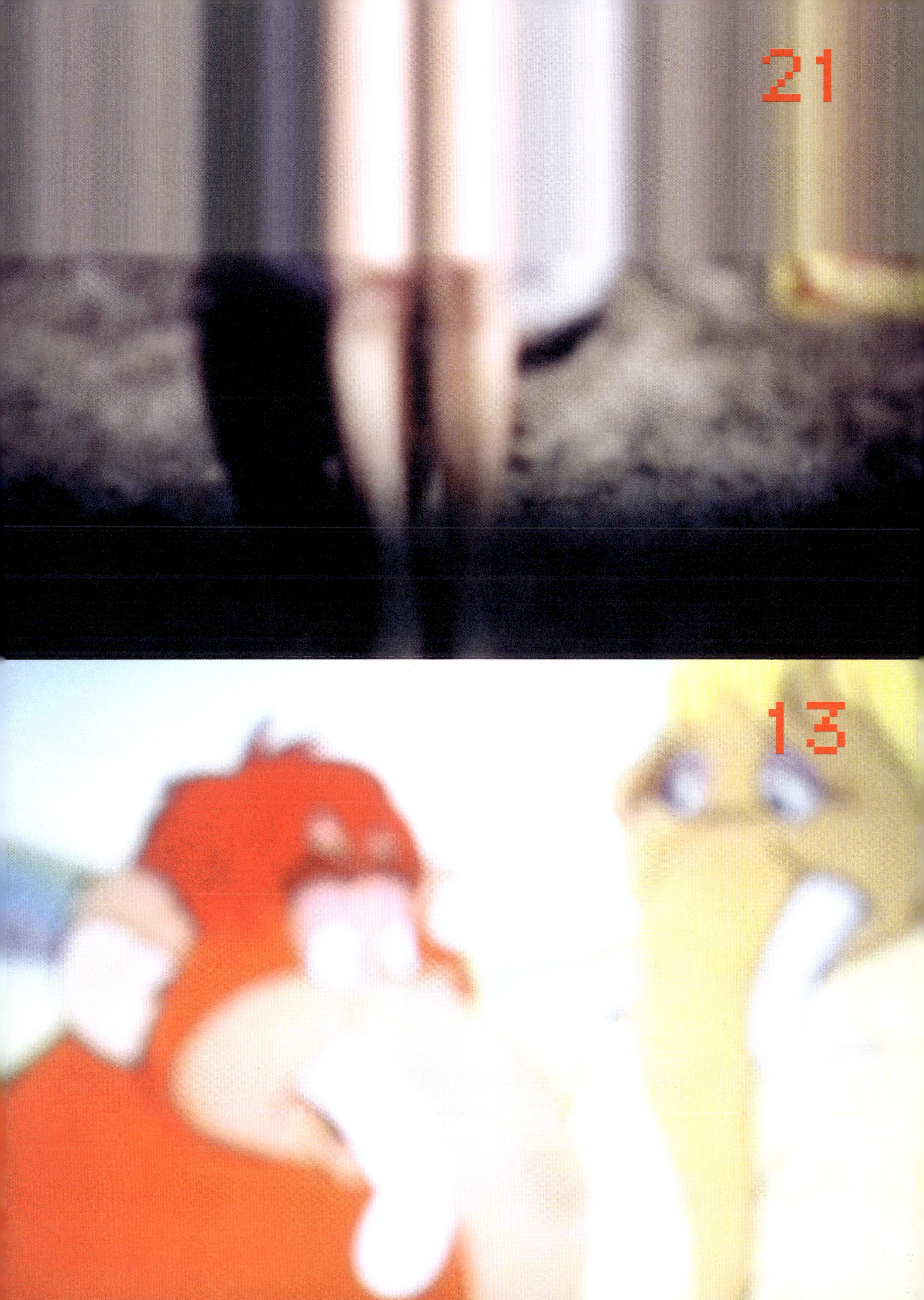
21
13

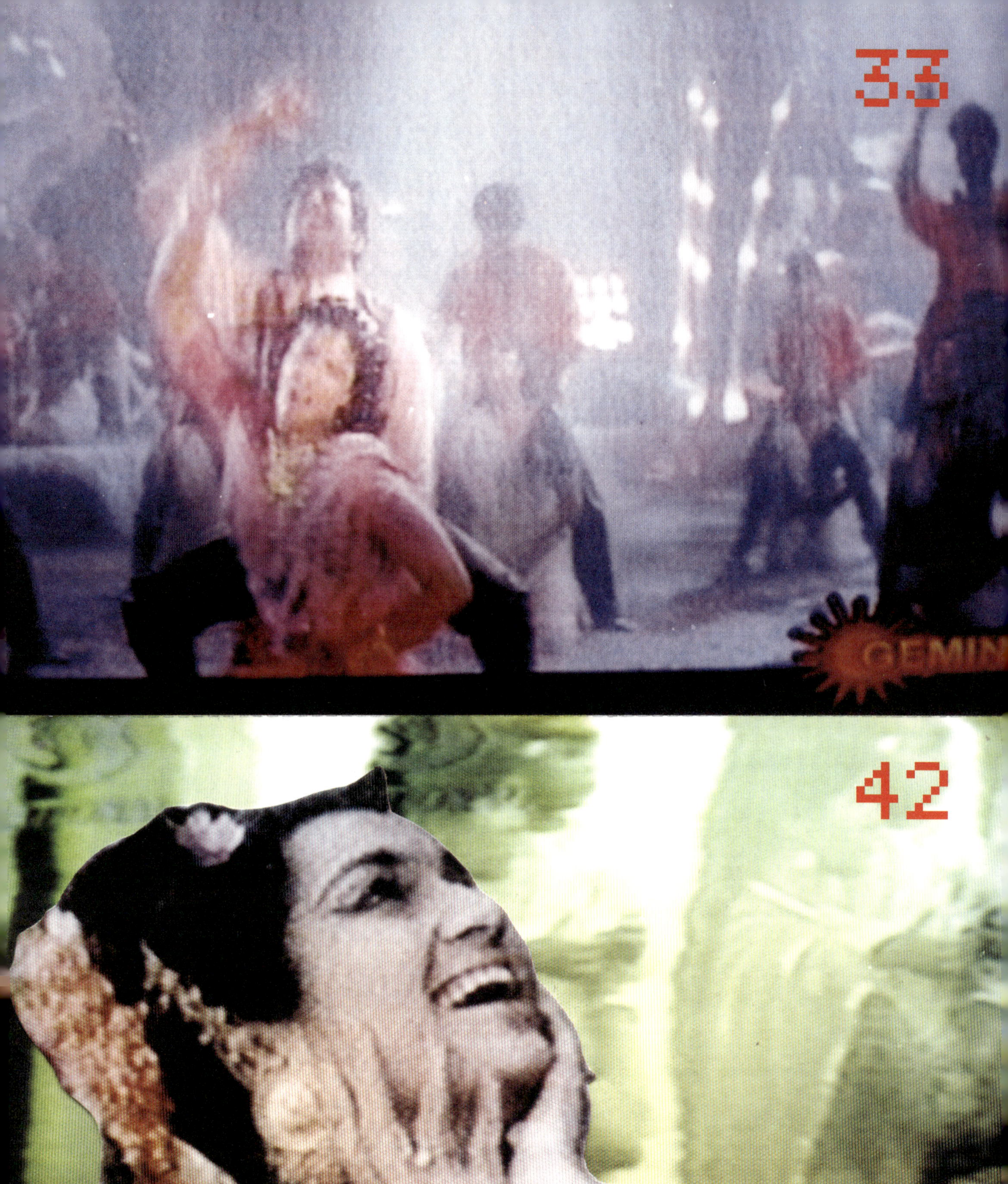
33
GEMIN
42

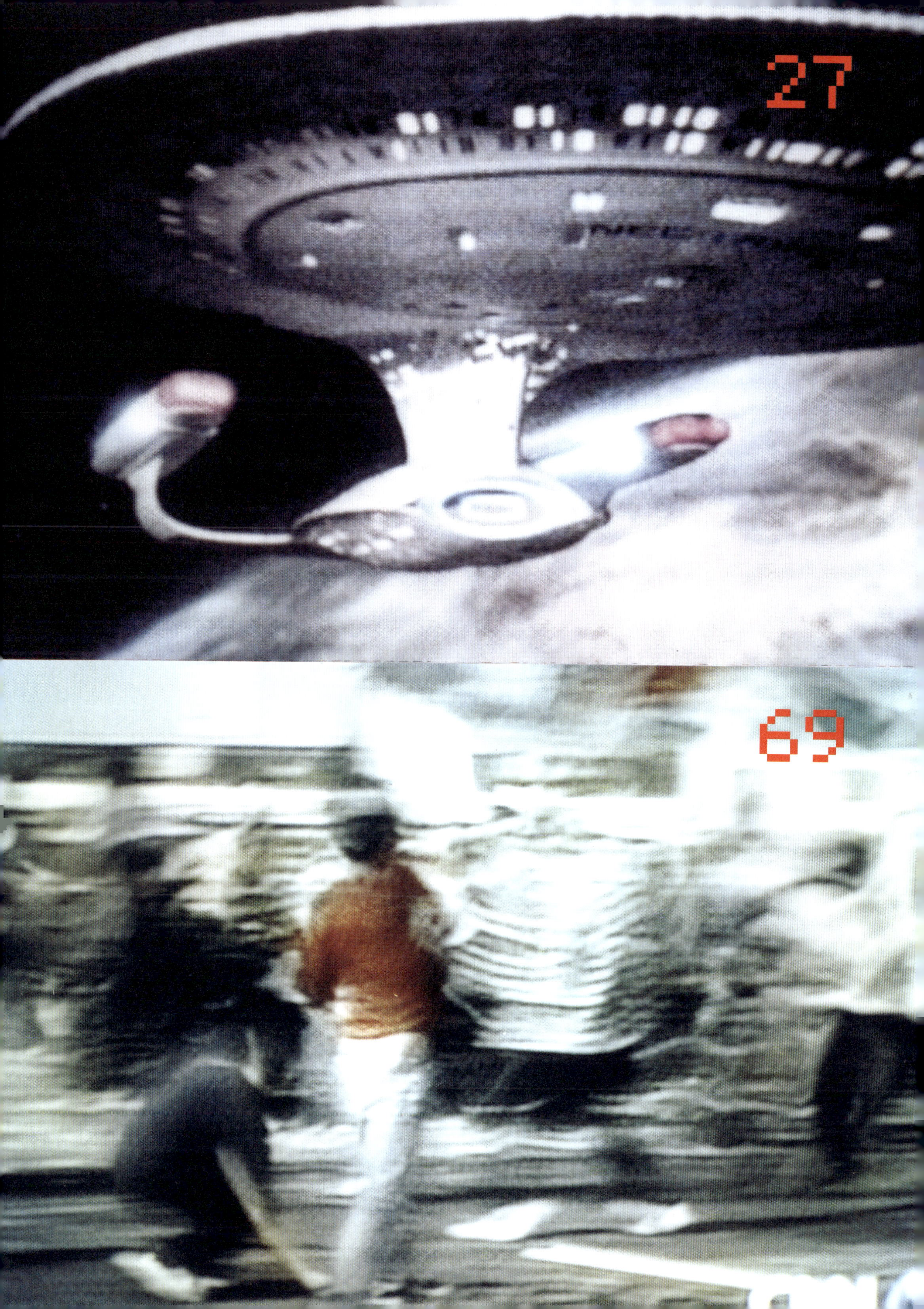
27
69

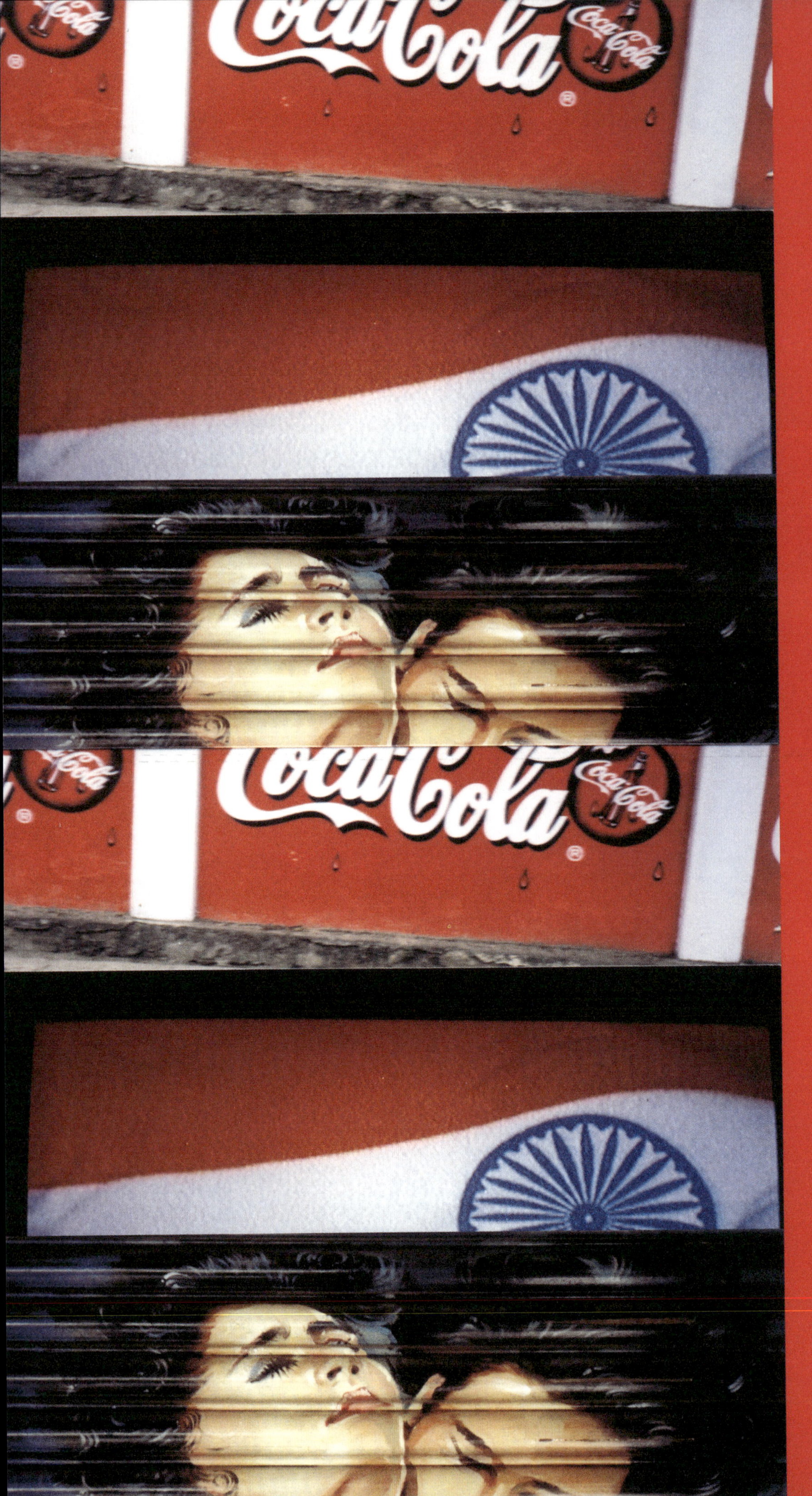
Coca-Cola
Coca-Cola

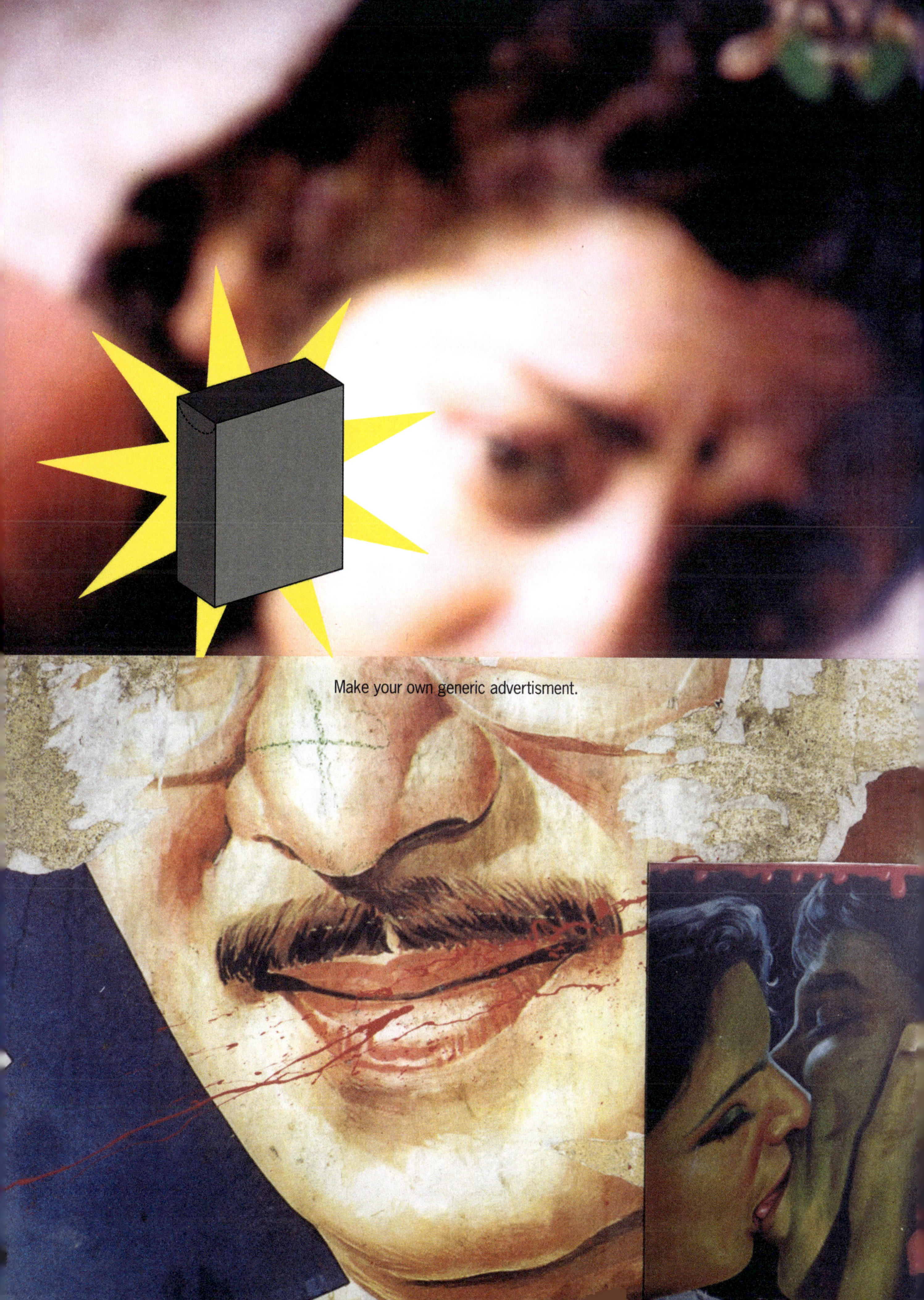
Make your own generic advertisment.

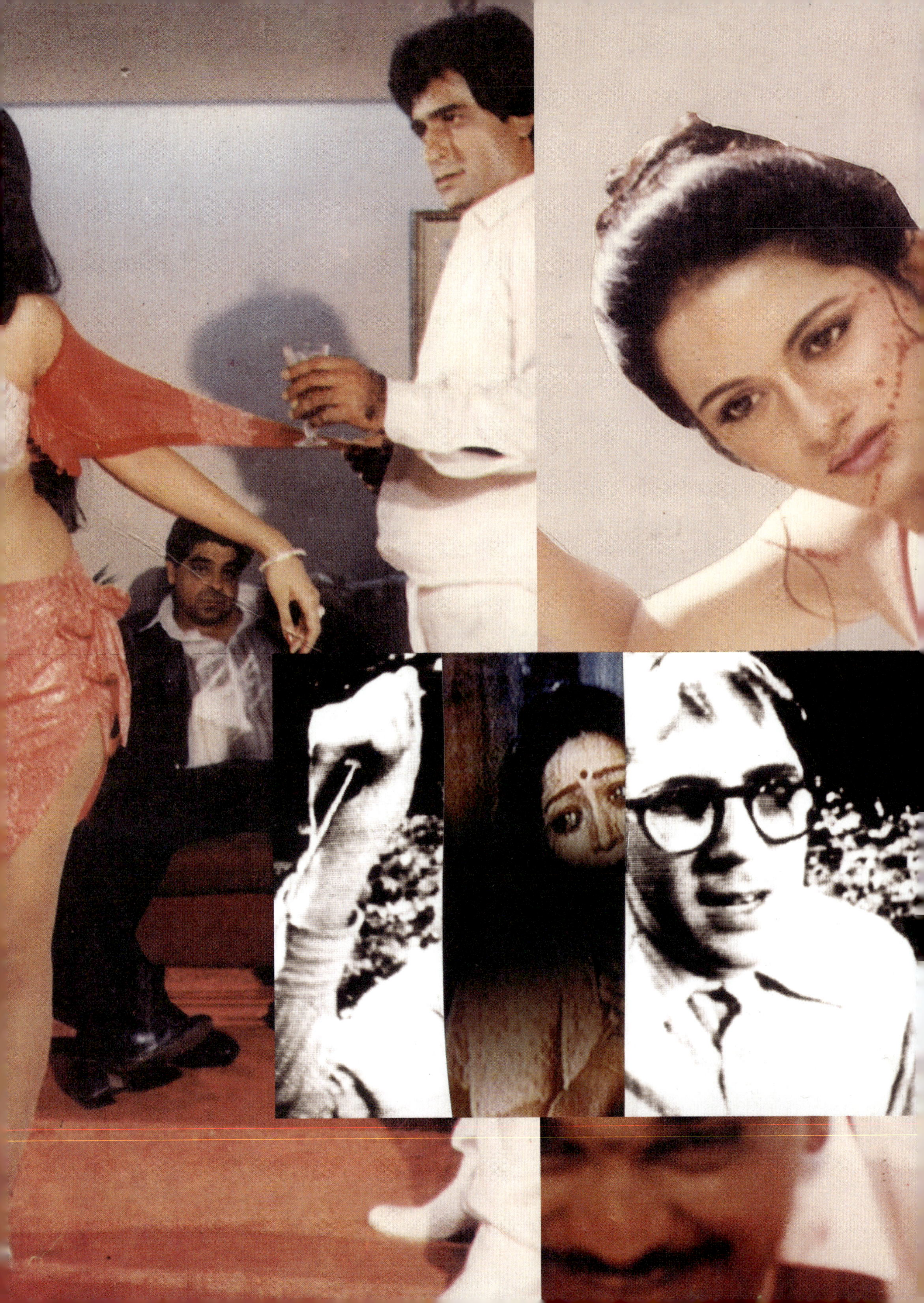

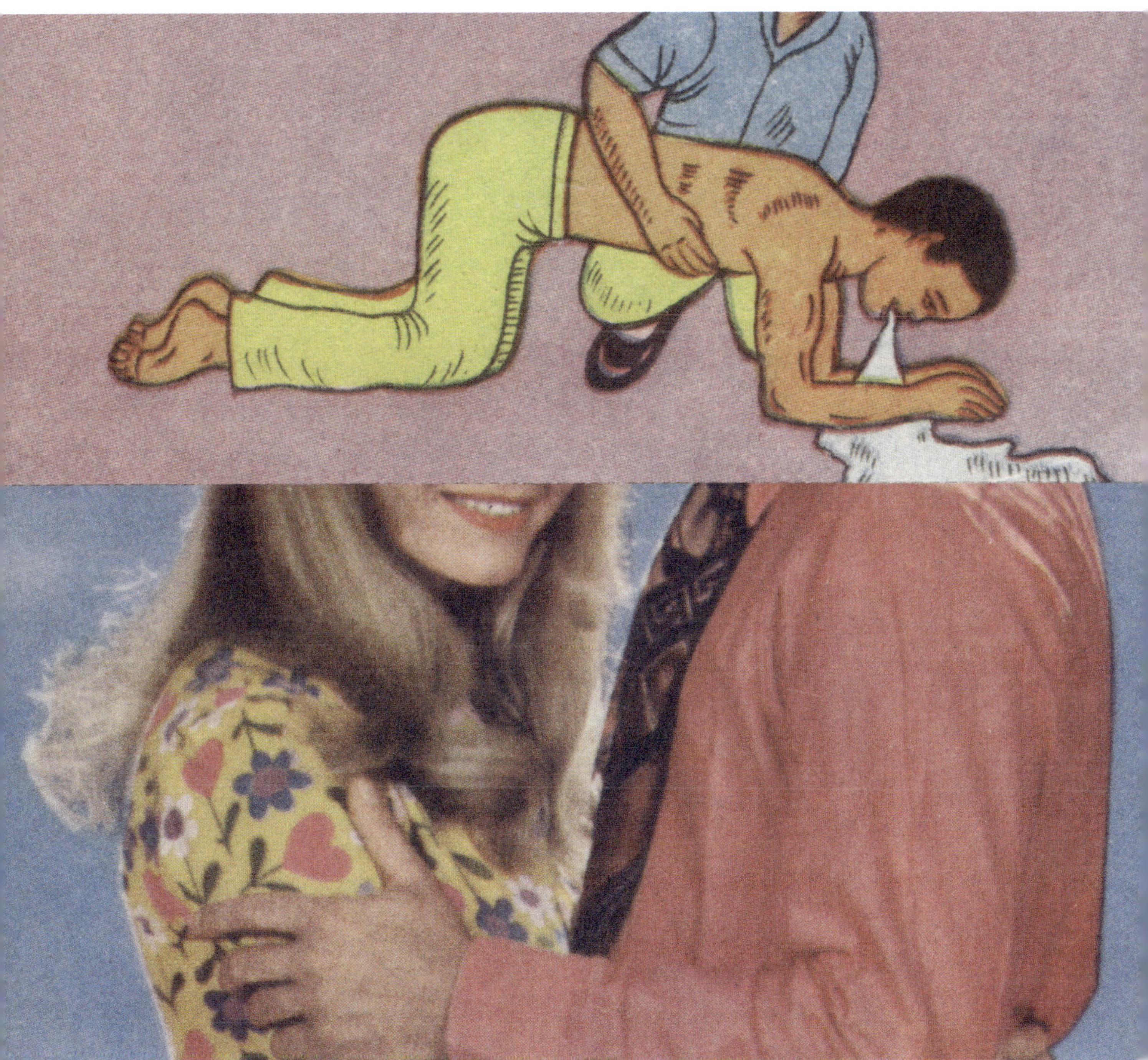

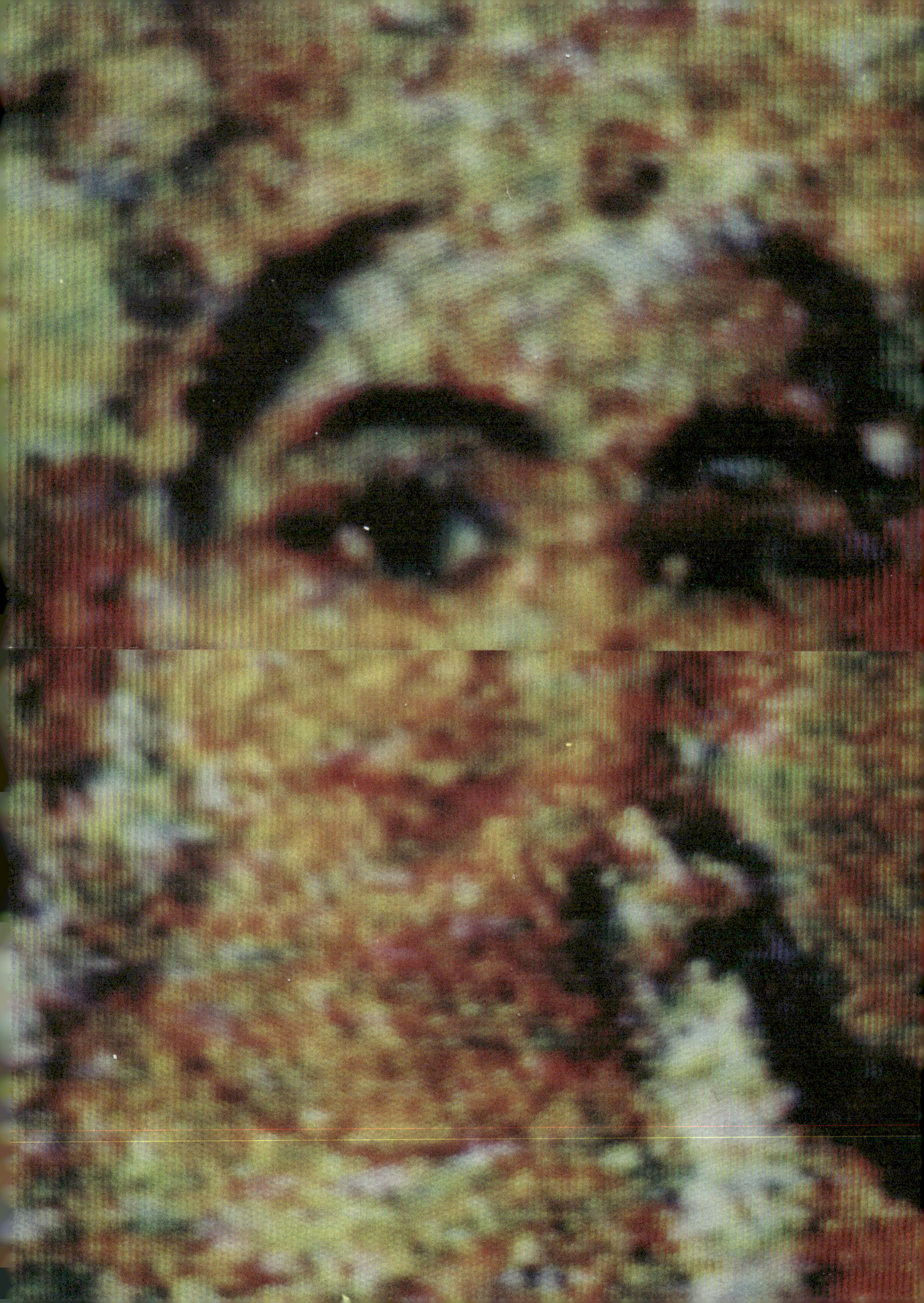

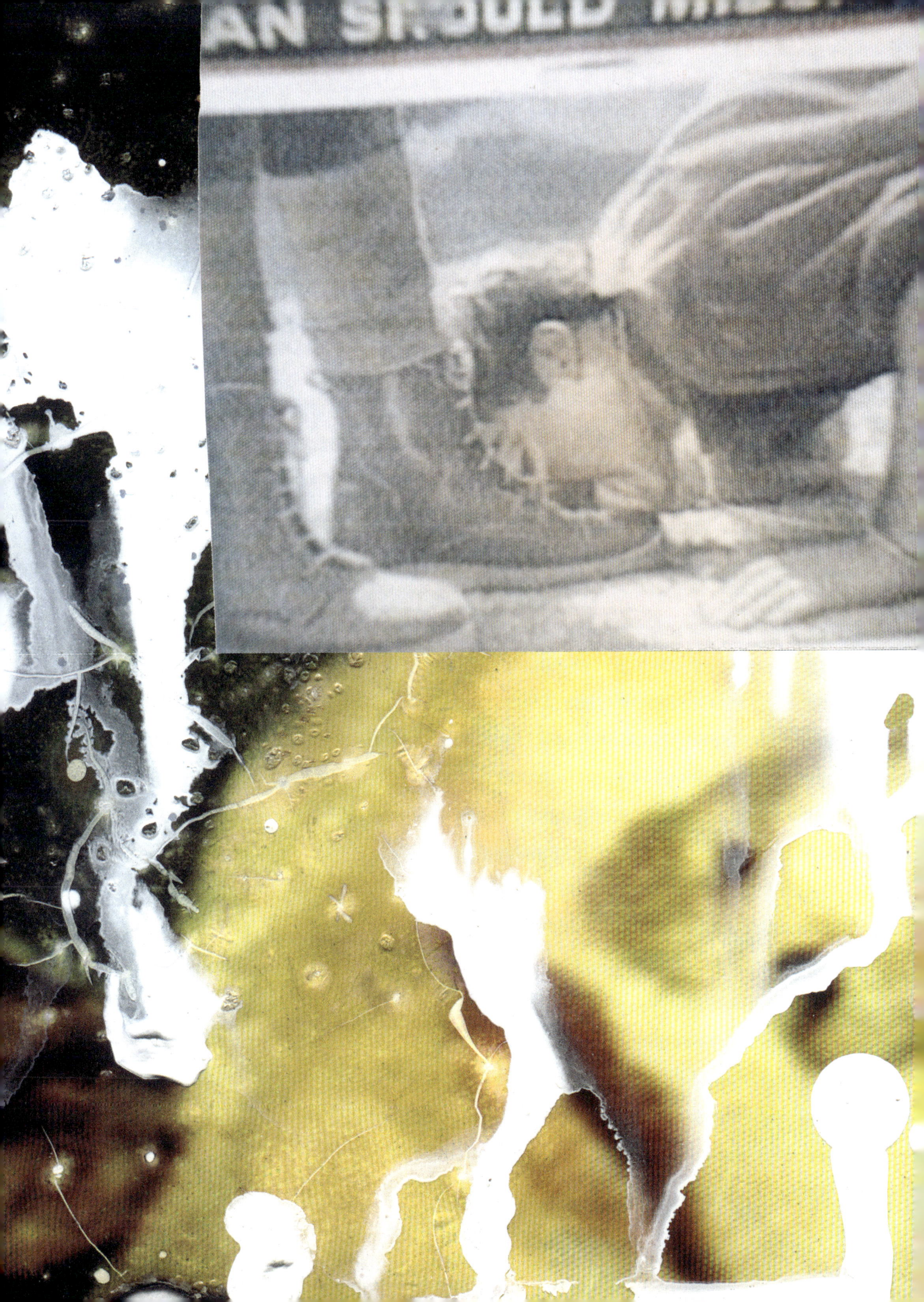

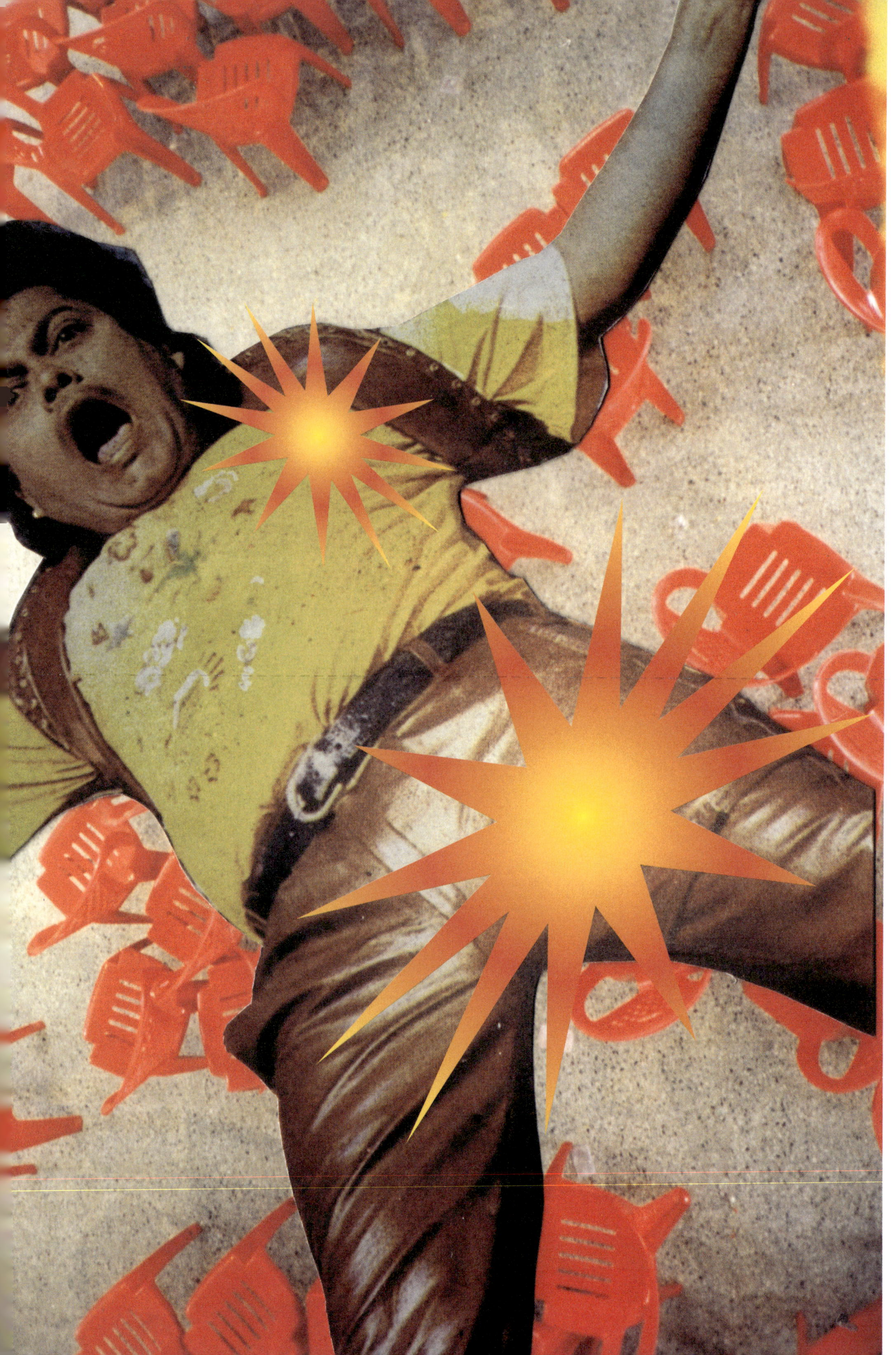

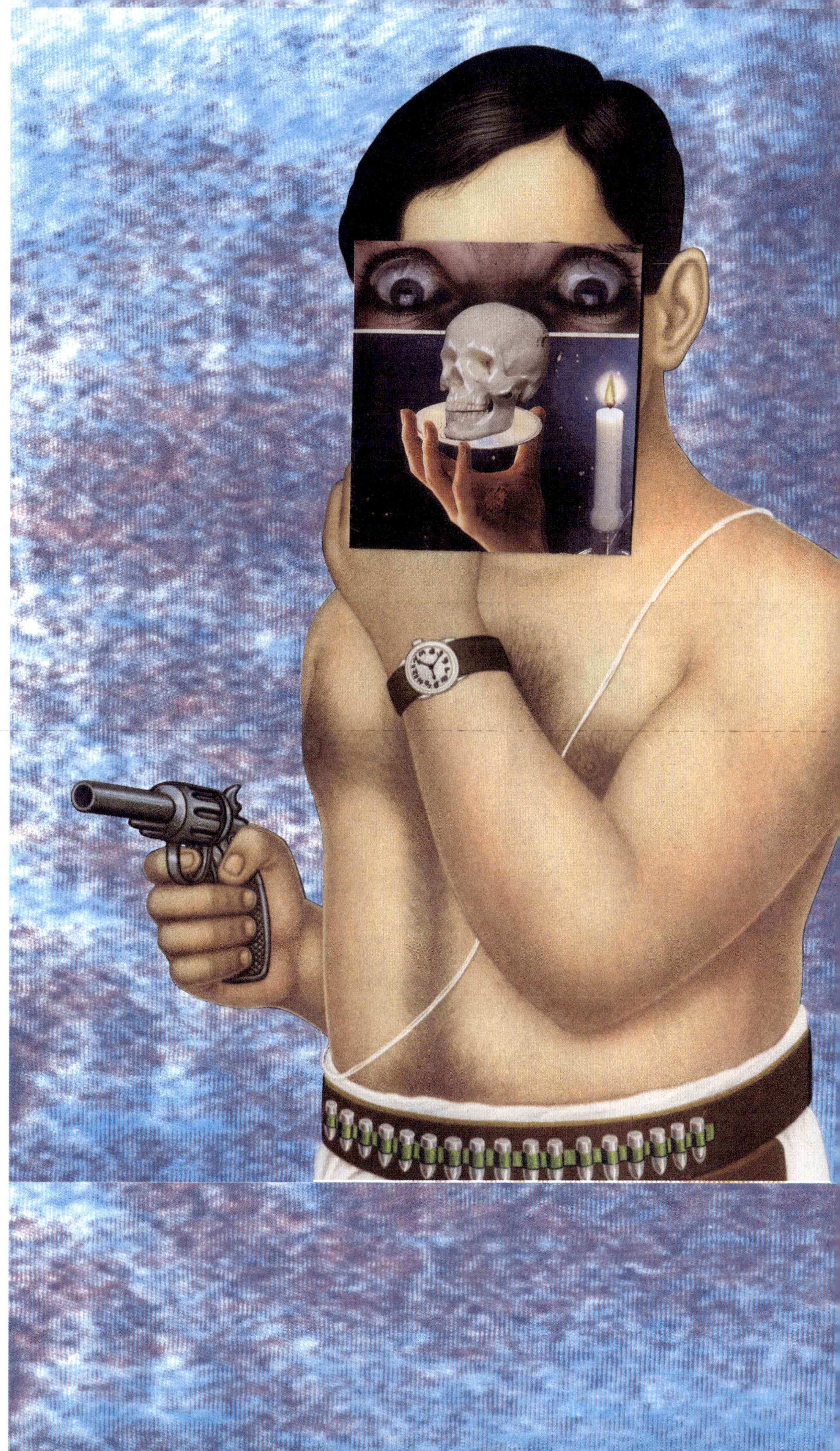

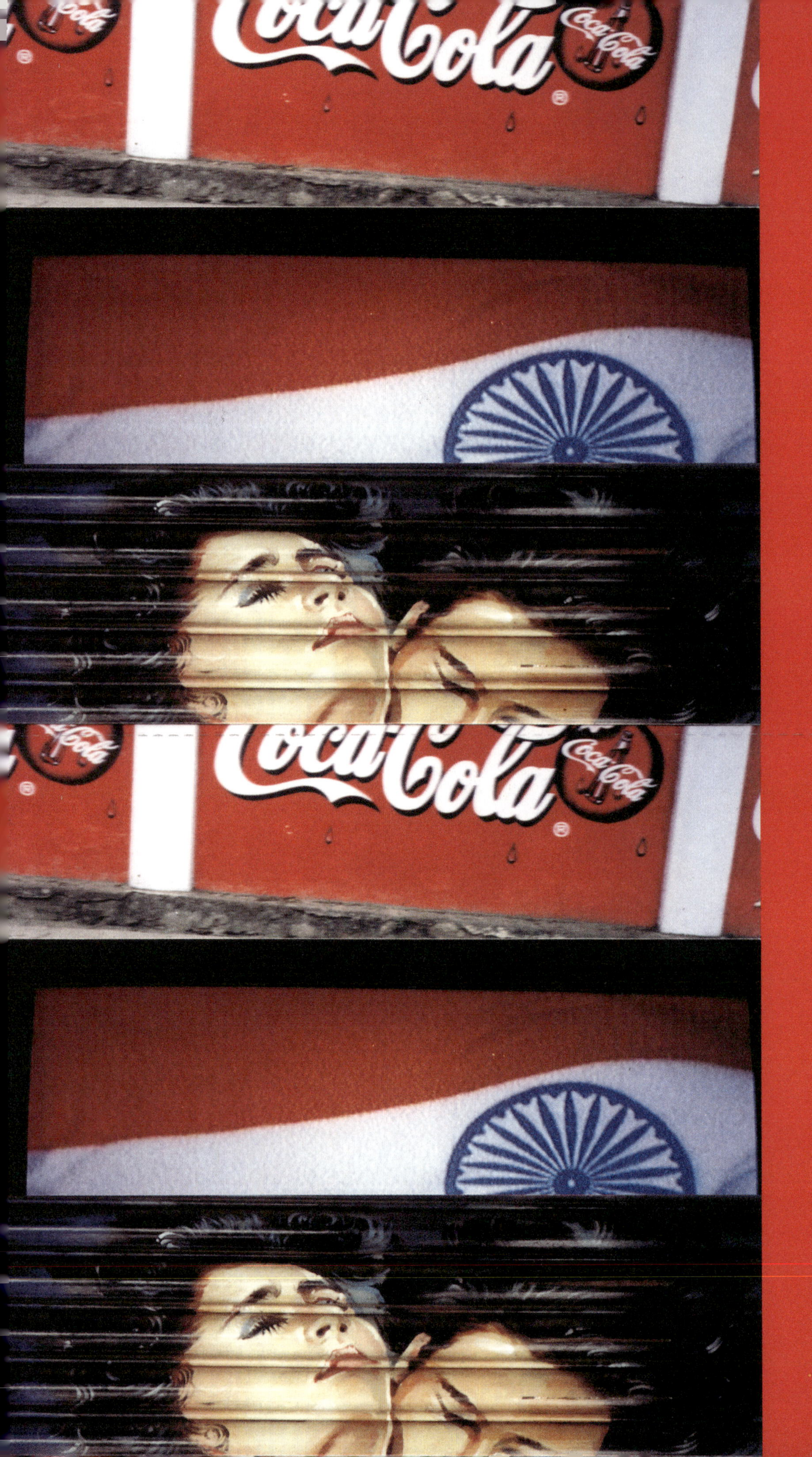
Coca-Cola
Coca-Cola

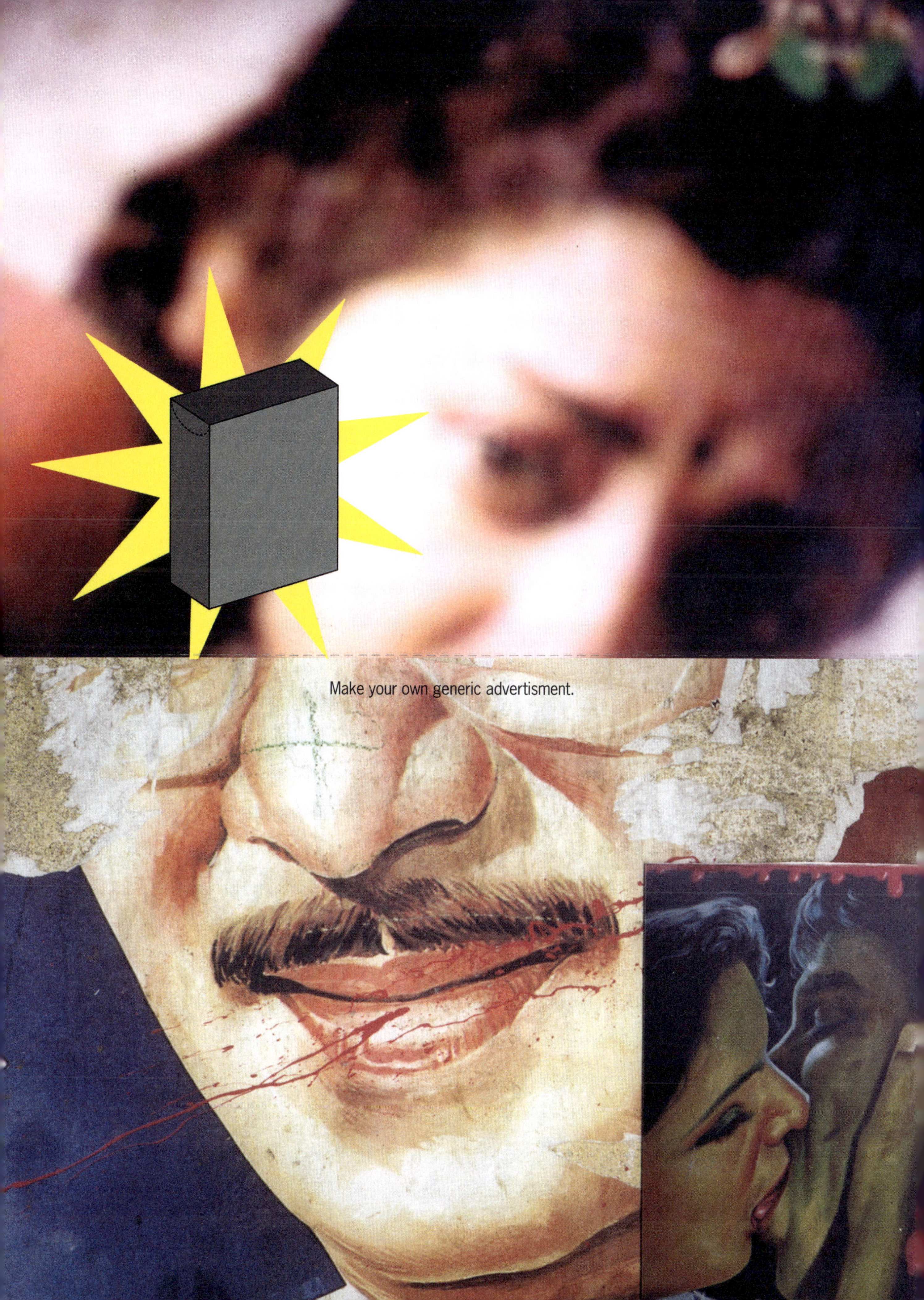
Make your own generic advertisment.

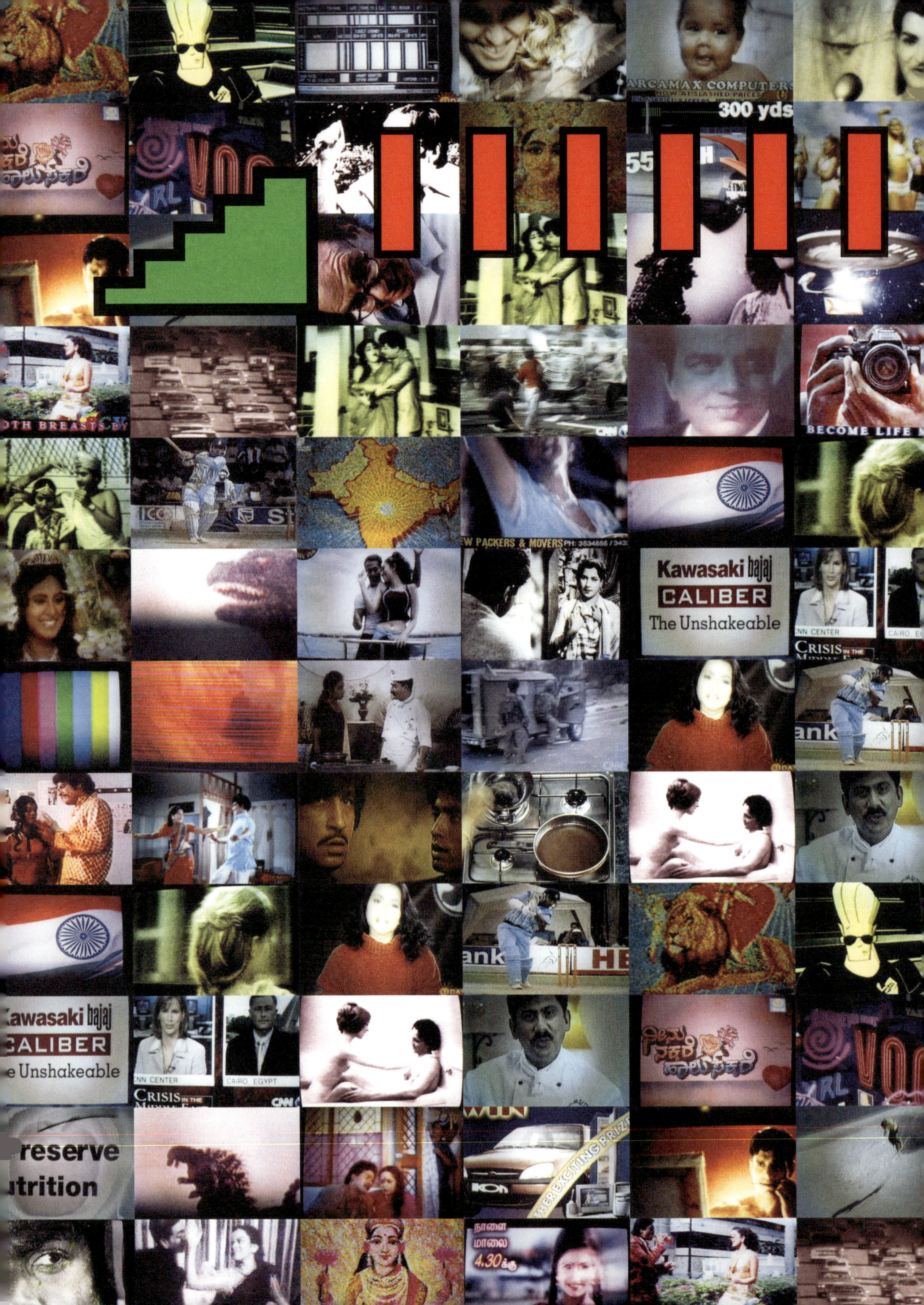
ARCAMAX COMPUTERS
NOW AT SLASHED PRICES
300 yds
OTH BREASTS BY
BECOME LIFE
EW PACKERS & MOVERS PH: 3534855 / 343
Kawasaki bajaj
CALIBER
The Unshakeable
NN CENTER
CRISIS IN THE
ank
ank
HE
awasaki bajaj
ALIBER
e Unshakeable
NN CENTER
CAIRO, EGYPT
CRISIS IN THE
reserve
utrition
WIN
THE EXCITING PRIZE
நாளை
மாலை
4.30க்கு

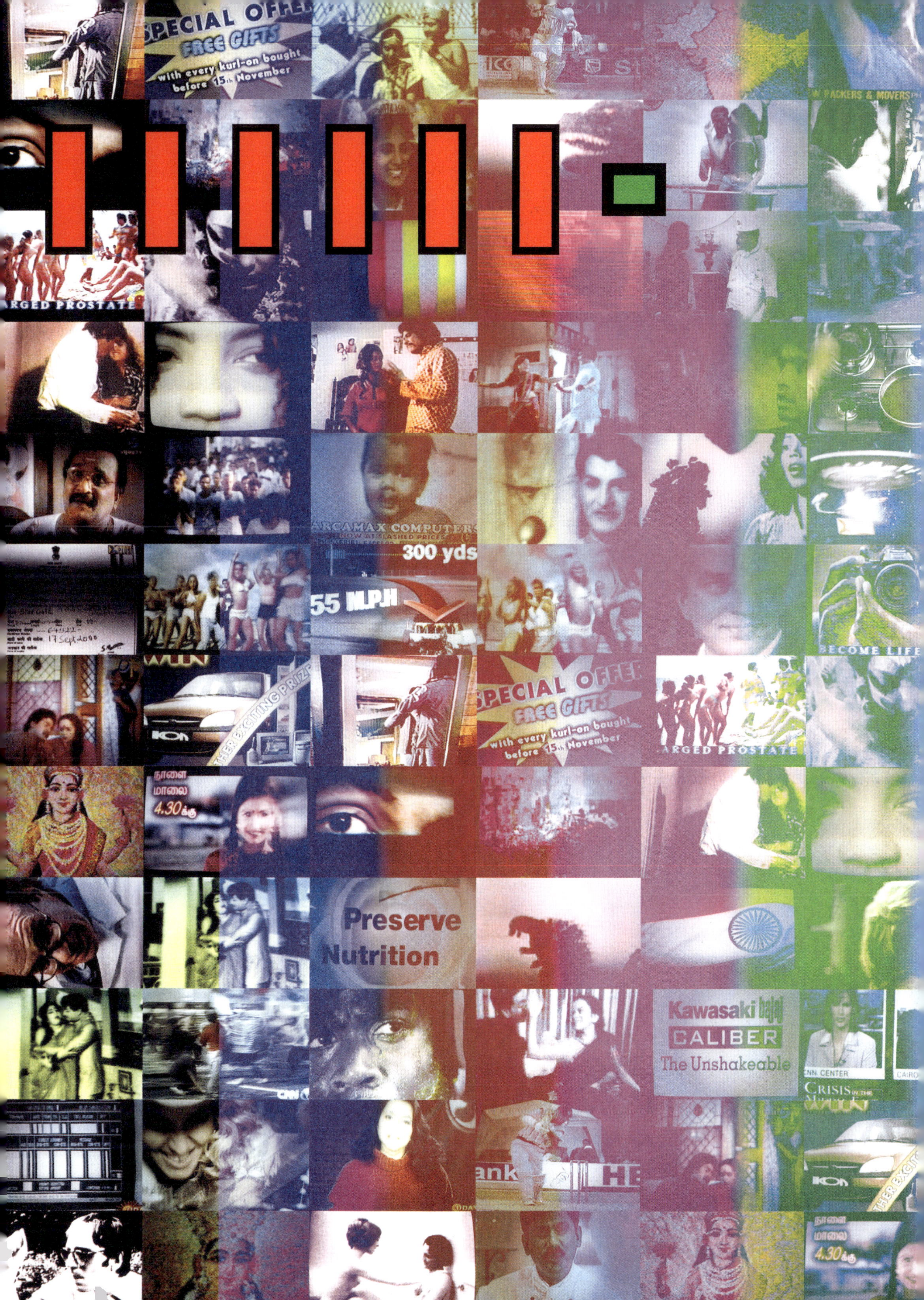
SPECIAL OFFER
FREE GIFTS
with every kurl-on bought before 15th November
PACKERS & MOVERS
ARGED PROSTATE
ARCAMAX COMPUTERS
300 yds
55 M.P.H
BECOME LIFE
THE EXCITING PRIZE
நாளை
மாலை
4.30க்கு
Preserve
Nutrition
Kawasaki bajaj
CALIBER
The Unshakeable
CNN CENTER
CRISIS

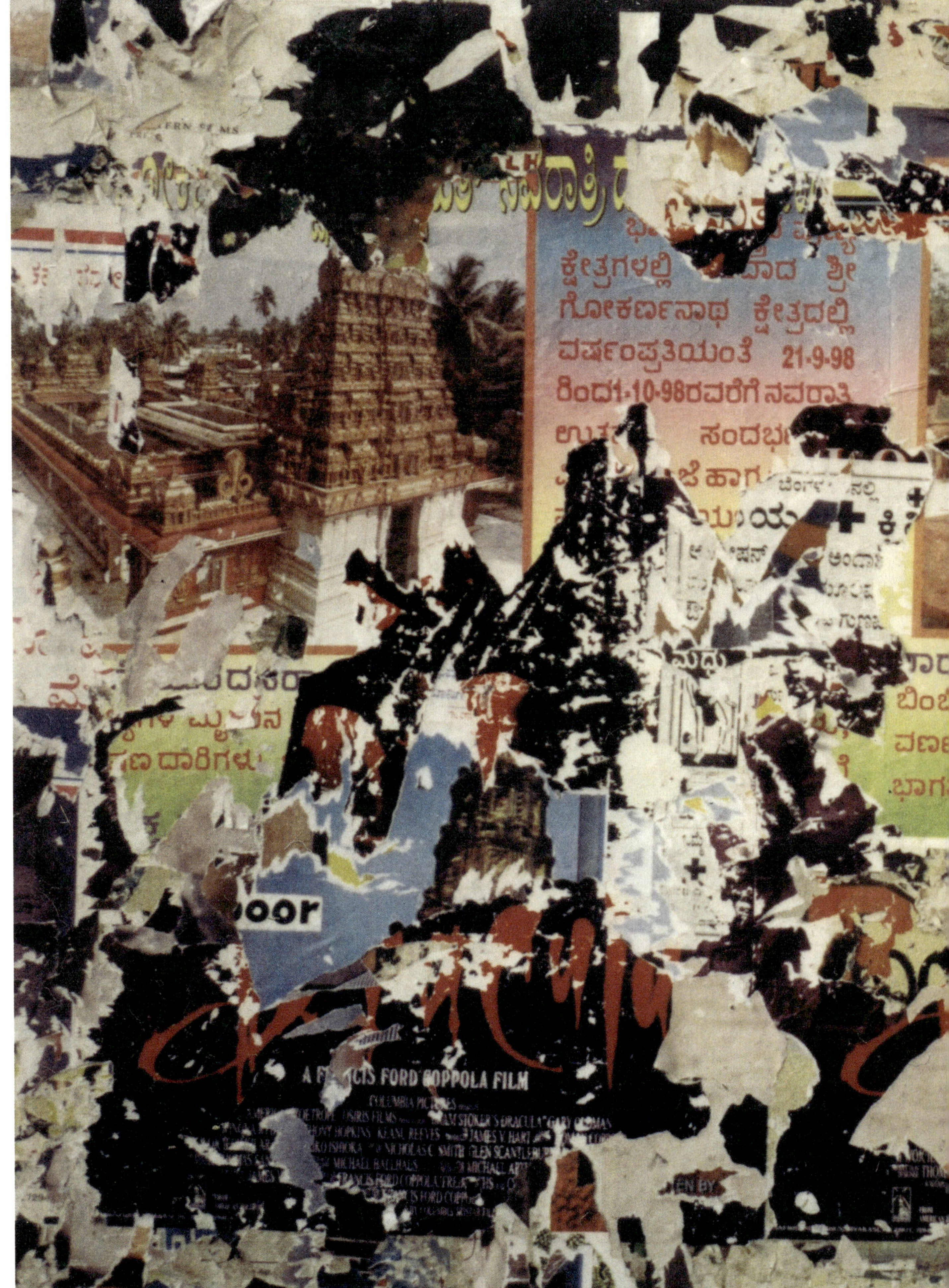
ಕ್ಷೇತ್ರಗಳಲ್ಲಿ
ಗೋಕರ್ಣನಾಥ ಕ್ಷೇತ್ರದಲ್ಲಿ
ವರ್ಷಂಪ್ರತಿಯಂತೆ 21-9-98
ಣದಾರಿಗಳು
oor
FORD COPPOLA FILM
COLUMBIA PICTURES

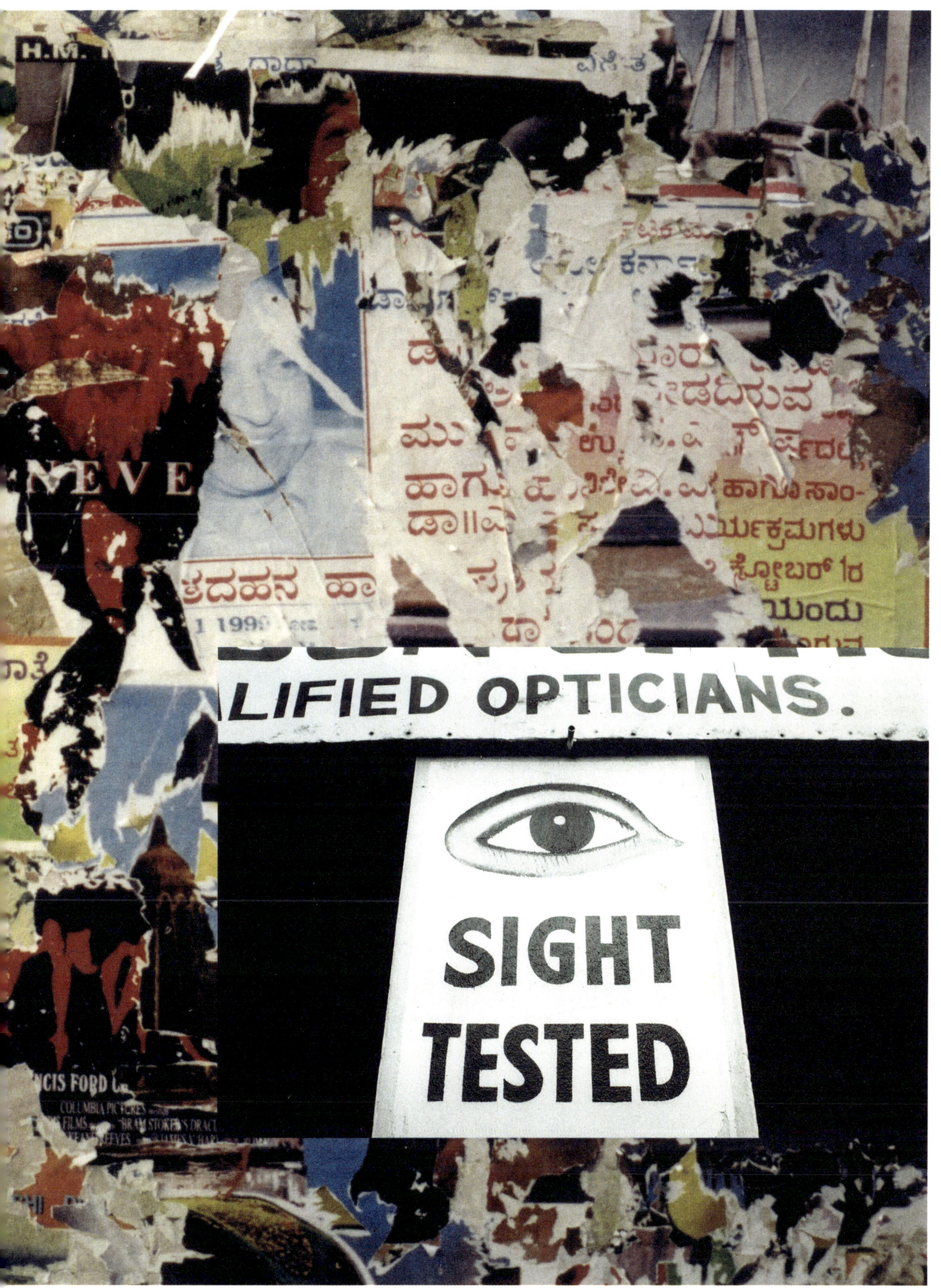
LIFIED OPTICIANS.
SIGHT
TESTED

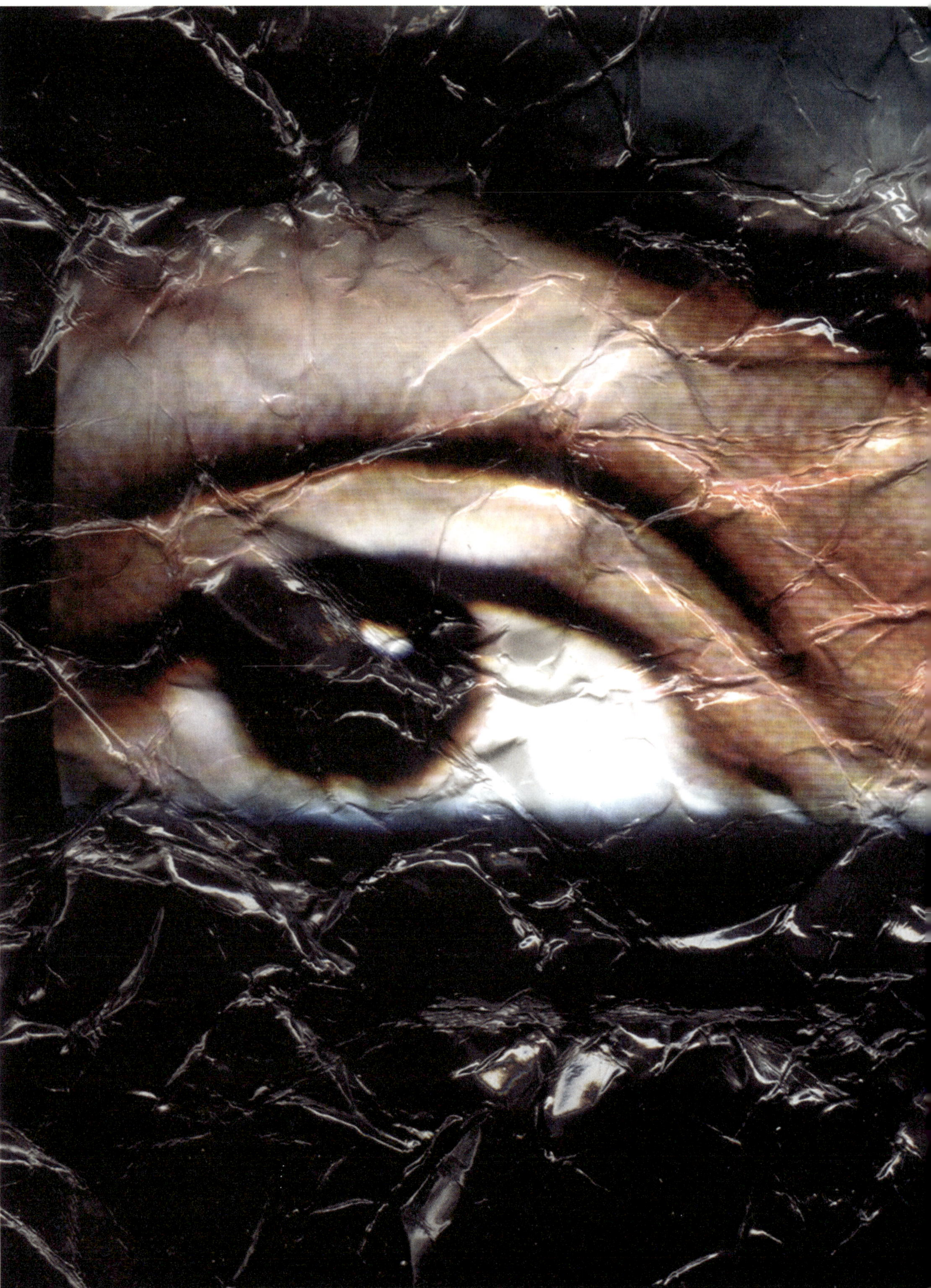

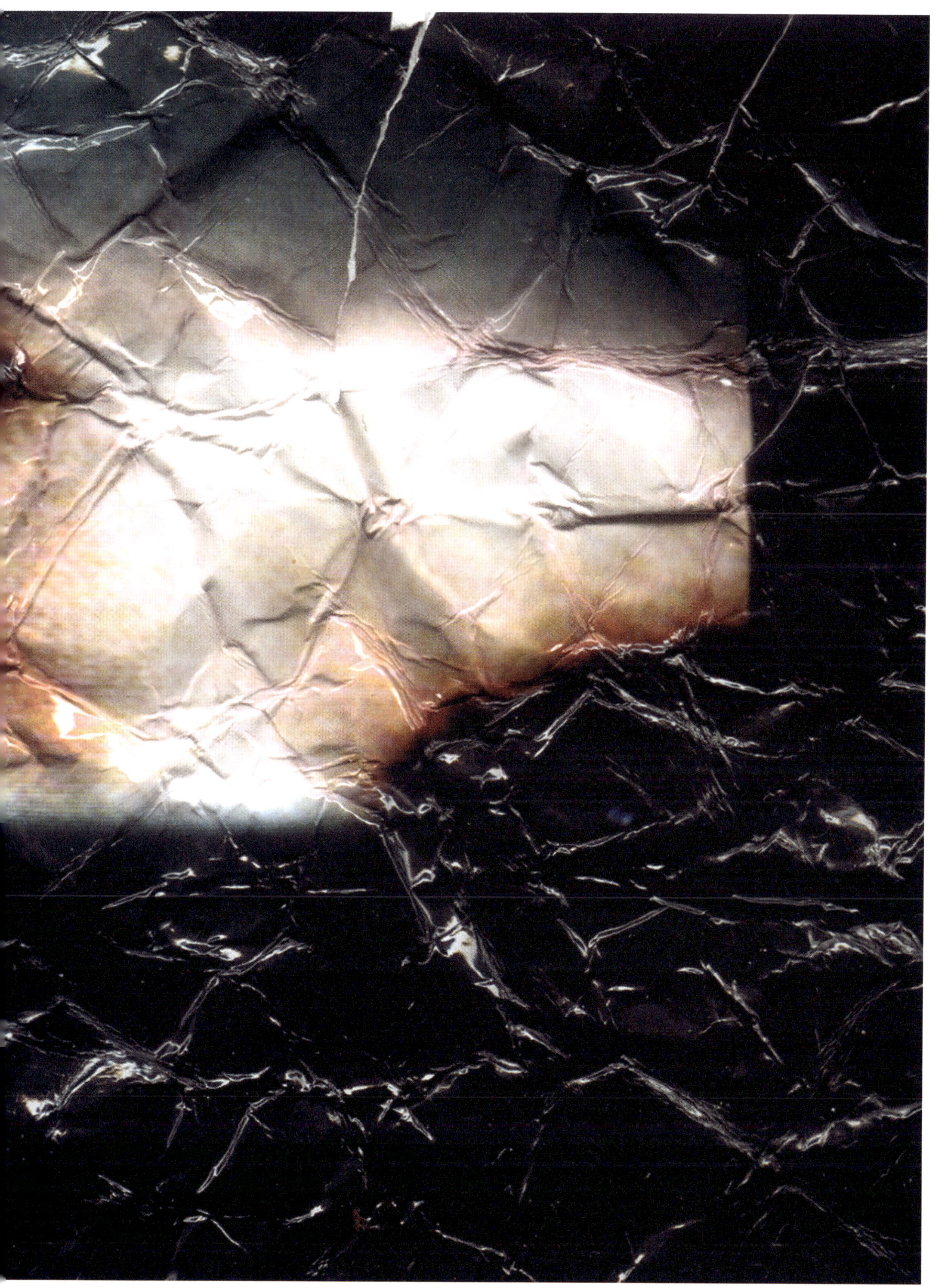

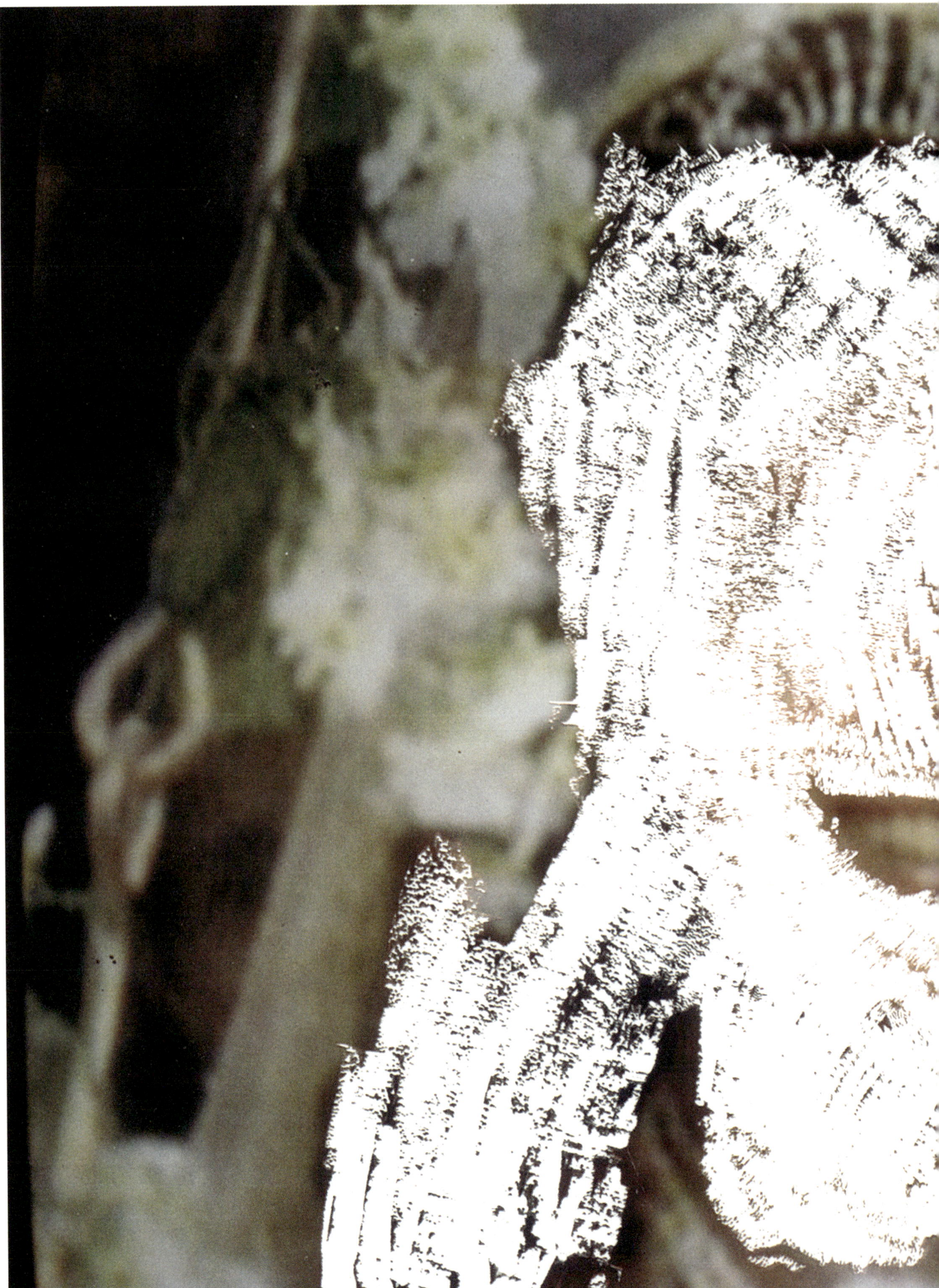

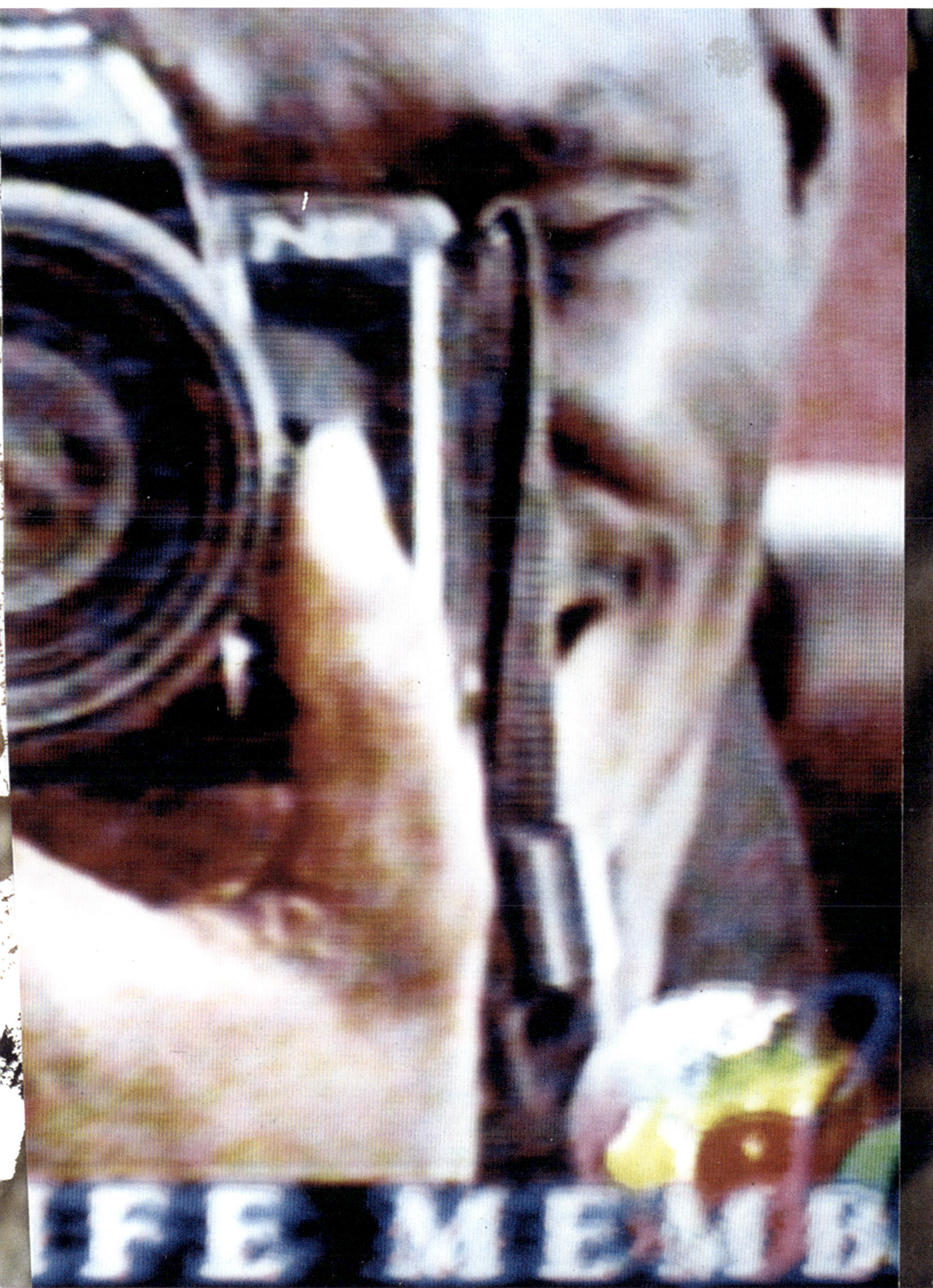
IFE MEMB

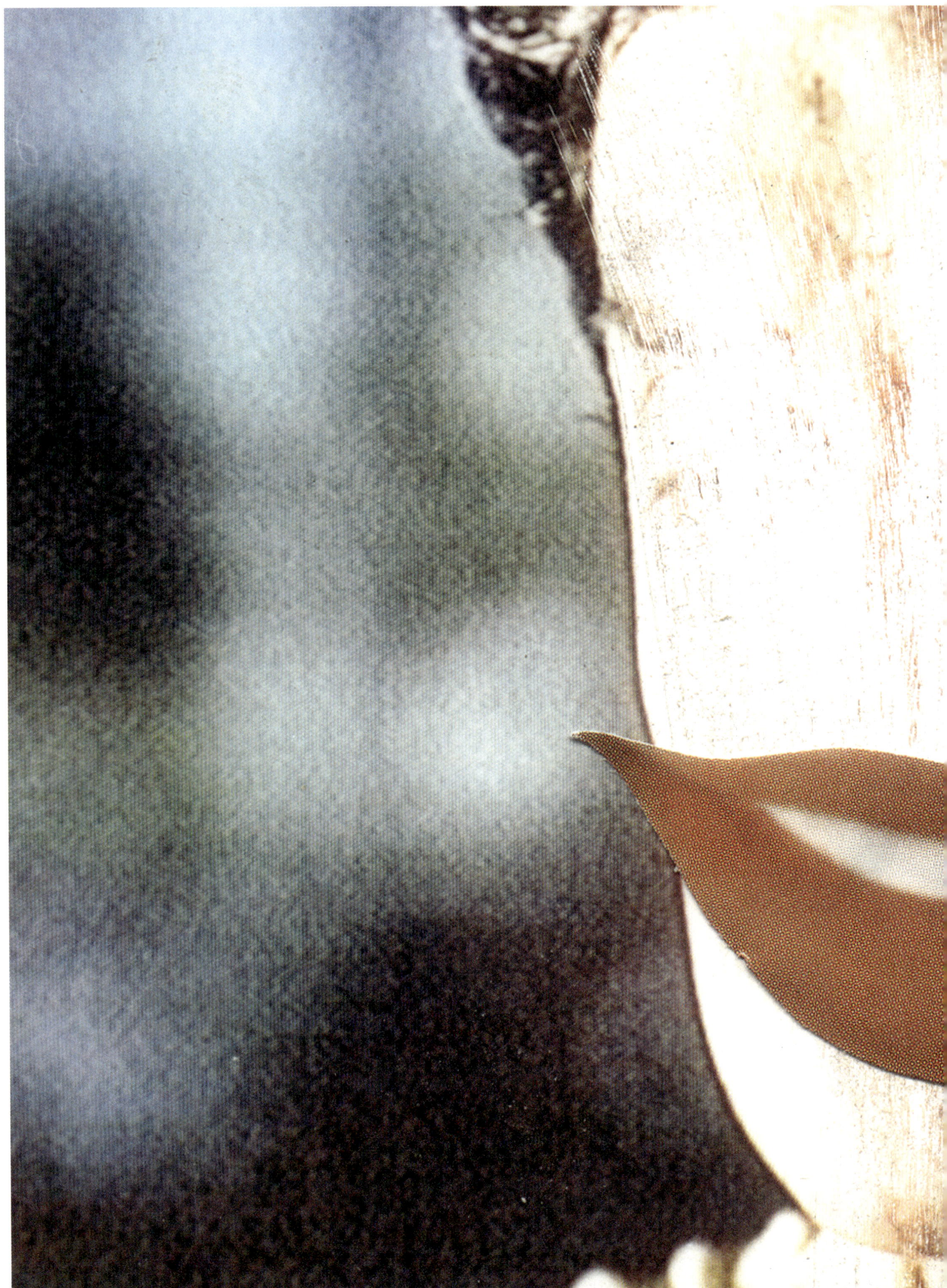

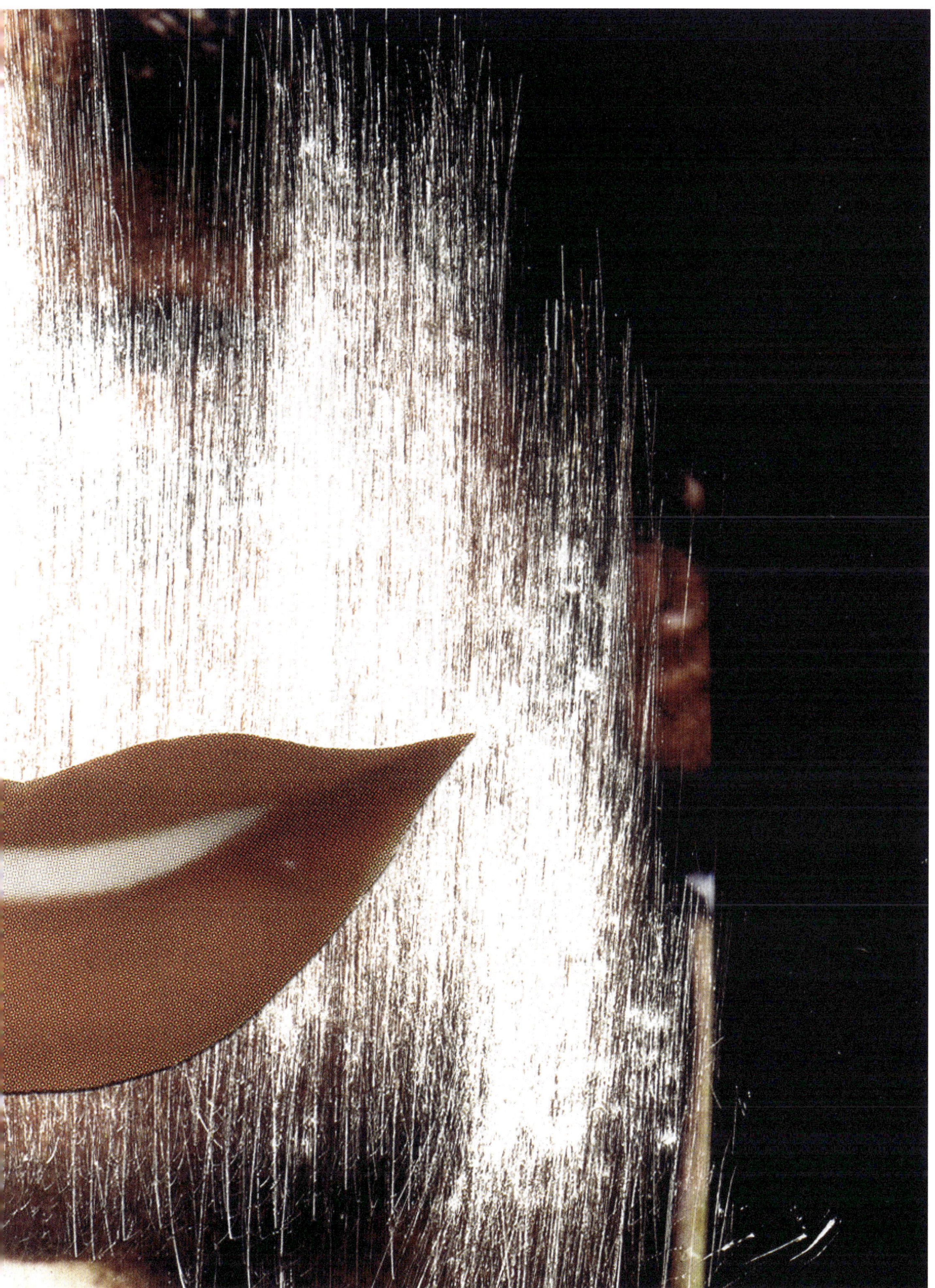

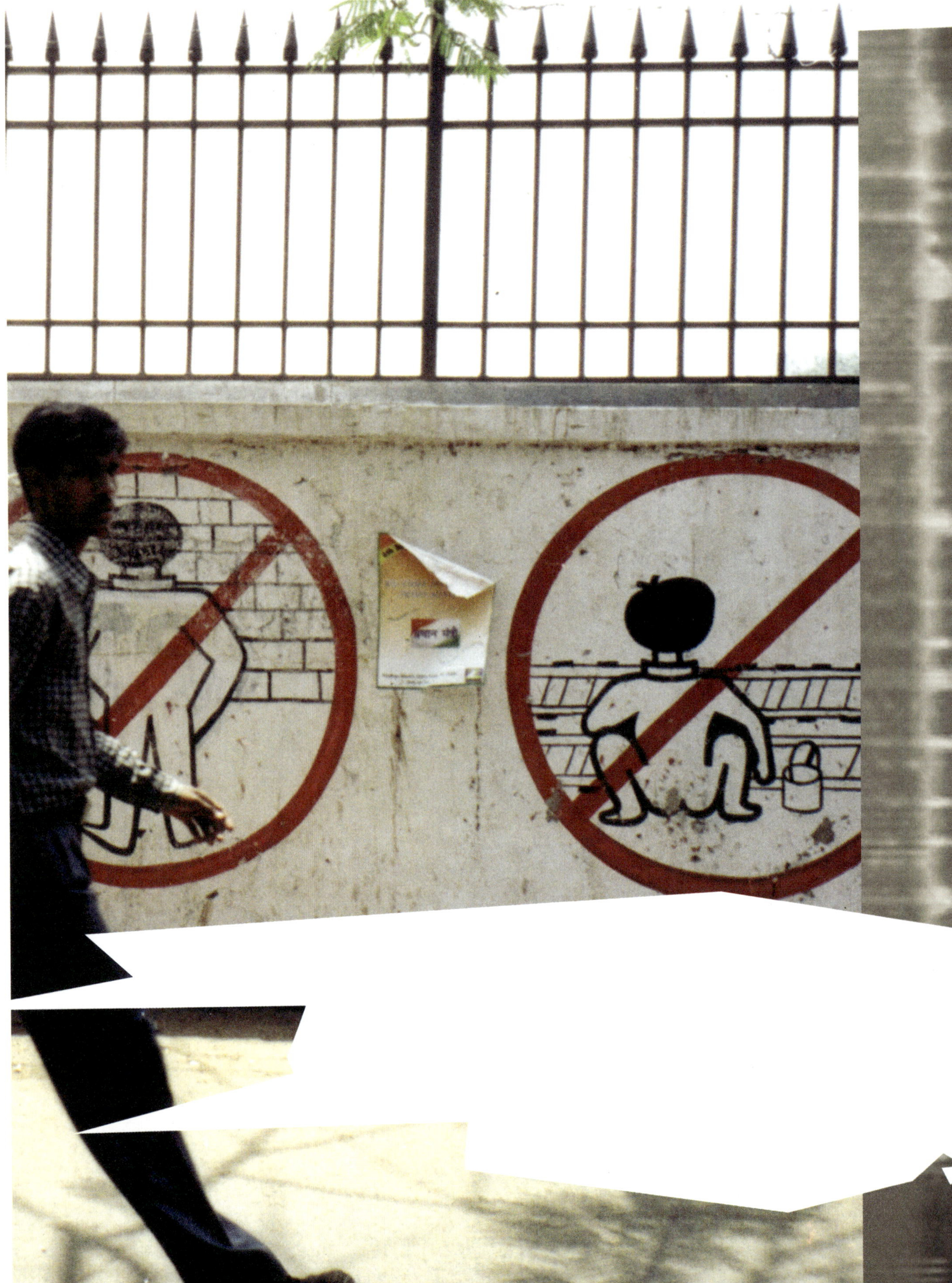

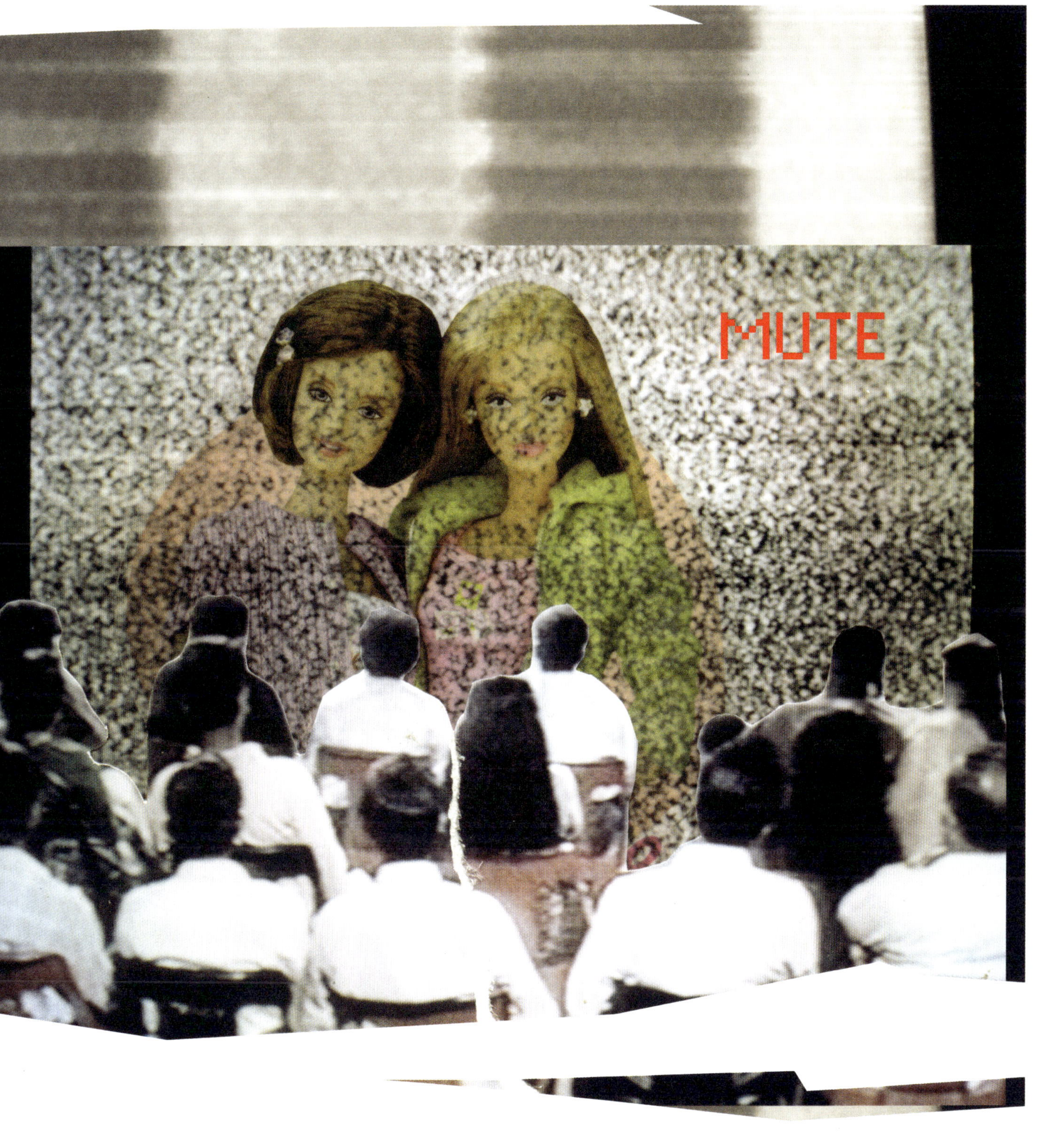
MUTE

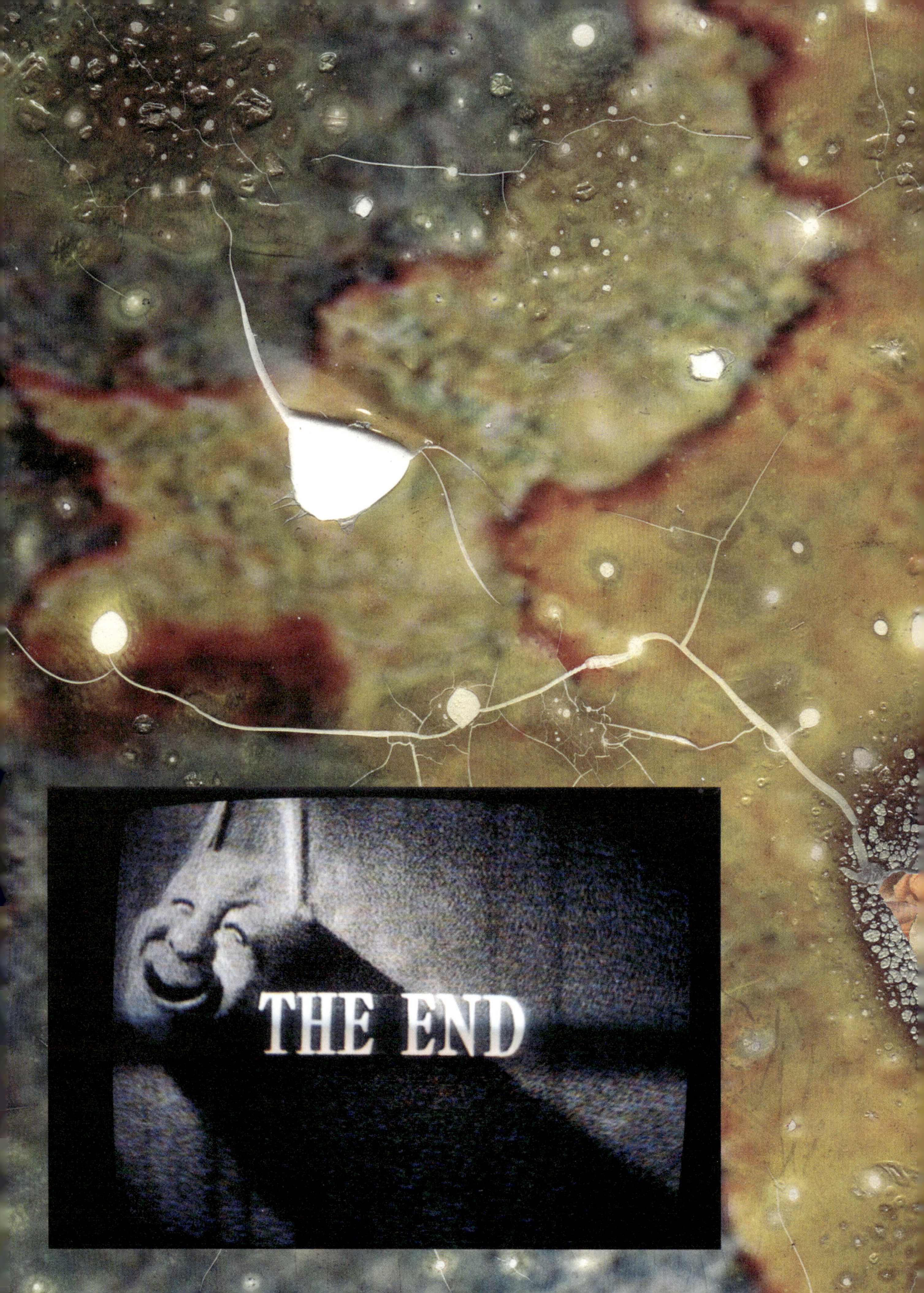
THE END

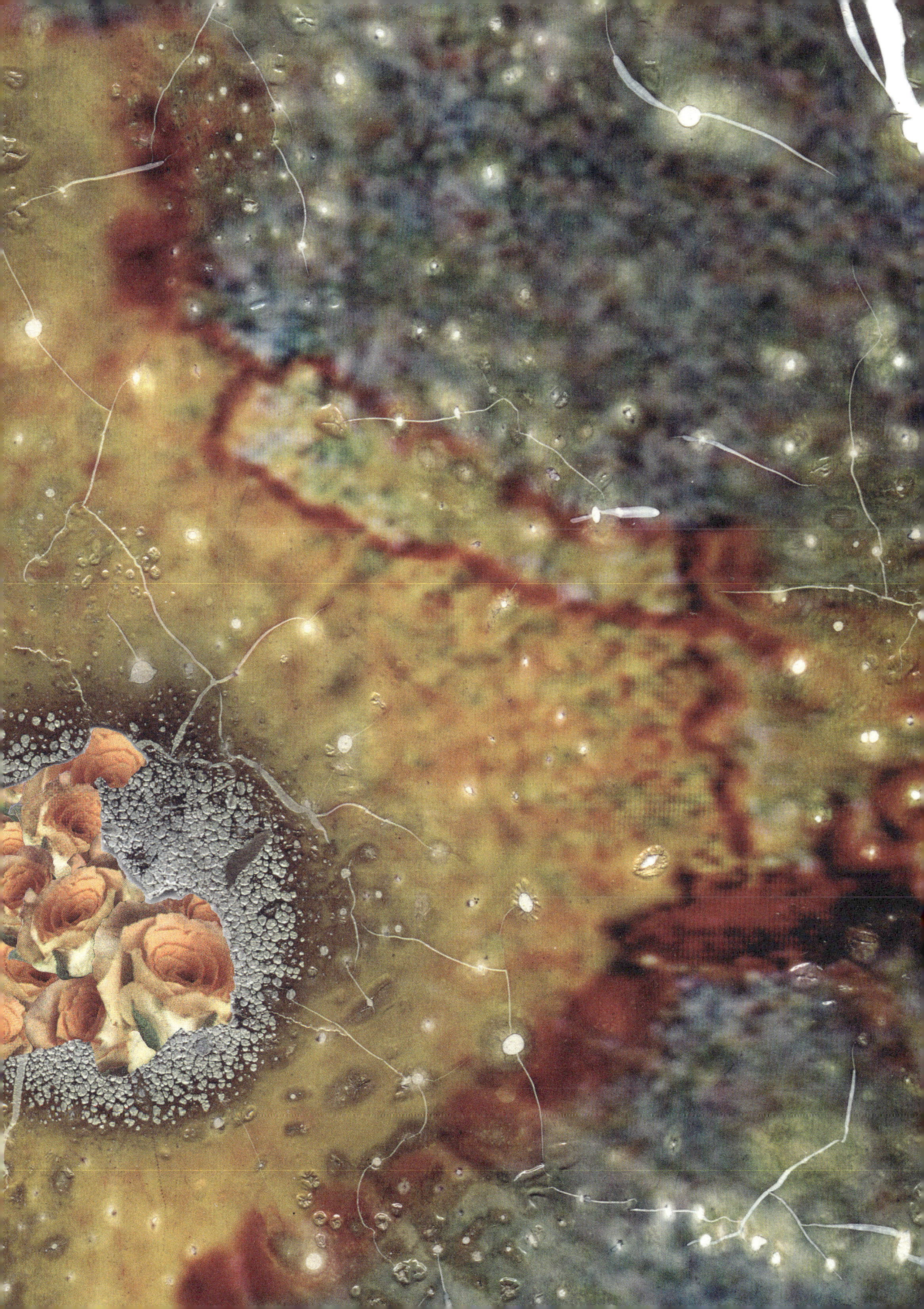

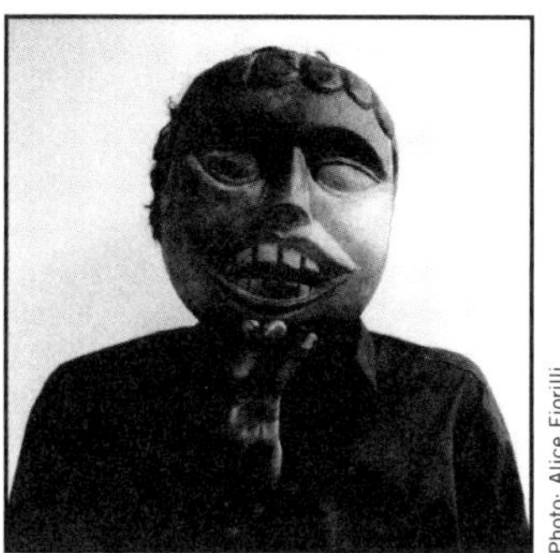

Photo: Alice Fiorilli

Avinash Veeraraghavan is a young artist living and working in Bangalore, India. He studied under the Italian designer Andrea Anastasio and worked for short periods at Studio Sowden and Studio Fronzoni in Milan. Avinash's work engages with a range of visual media from photography to installation. This book marks his interest in popular culture and in exploring the nature of the psyche that produces it.

I LOVE MY INDIA

For this edition: Tara Publishing and Dewi Lewis Publishing

Printed and bound at Sirivatana Interprint PCL., Thailand

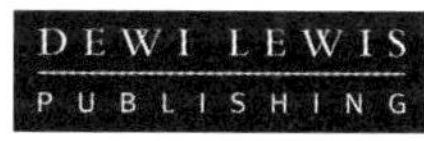

www.dewilewispublishing.com

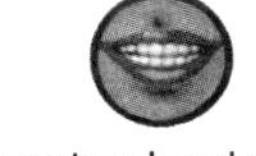

www.tarabooks.com

ISBN: 81-86211-65-9

OTHER TITLES ON INDIAN POPULAR CULTURE

"Jeff Koons meets Gilbert and George in this sure-fire number one smash hit."

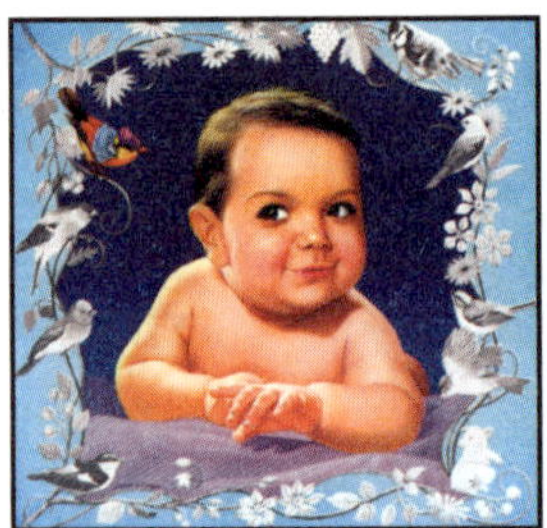

Hardback, 104 pages
7x7 inches, colour
ISBN: 1-904587-01-1
UK £11.99 / US $18

Baby!

Doctor Baby, Agriculture Baby, Apollo Baby, Army Baby ... bought by millions of people, painted baby posters are a household feature in India. Featuring one hundred classic baby posters, this extravagant book is unashamedly zany.

"Simply divine. Sirish Rao turns the pages on the nation's family album." – **The Guardian Weekend**

"Unbelievably cute (and extremely trendy) ... Adorn your coffee table with this scrumptious, luscious book, that's as delicious as an Indian sweet centre in Eid." – **BBC Roots**

"Ah, those cultural differences, and how richer we all are for being able to share in them. Kick-start your biological clock with the help of these air-brush artisans of the East." – **Al Burian**

"A source book that every artist and illustrator should own. Big and glossy."

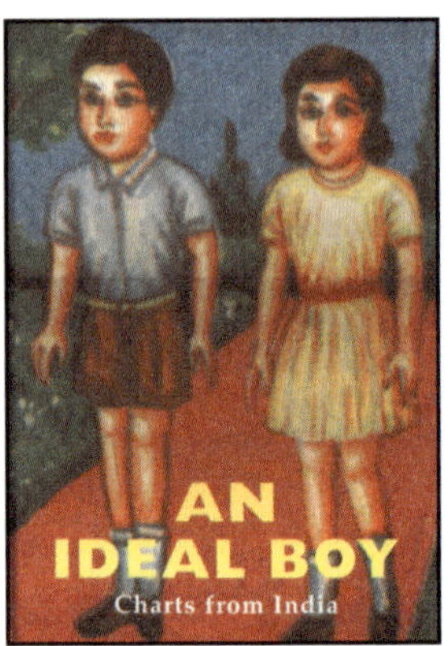

Hardback, 136 pages
13x9.5 inches, colour
ISBN: 1-899235-83-3
UK £19.99 / US $35

An Ideal Boy: Charts from India

This is a uniquely illuminating and hugely entertaining survey of a fascinating Indian phenomenon – charts. A mixture of stylised popular culture and sanctimonius pedagogy, these bold and lurid documents are a form of pre-politically correct communication that is startling to the outsider. This book is the first ever complete survey of charts, featuring examples going back decades.

"Drop those Bollywood breaks records now! Like a breath of fresh air into our airbrushed world of perfectionism, Indian charts draw you in with their endearingly cackhanded, kitsch and downright daft aesthetic." – **Lauren Cochrane, The Face Magazine**

"A delightful aspect of Indian pop culture ..." – **Paul Makovsky, Metropolis Magazine**

"One of the most comforting feel-good experiences available ... I defy anyone not to chuckle."
– **David Jenkins, The Sunday Telegraph Magazine**

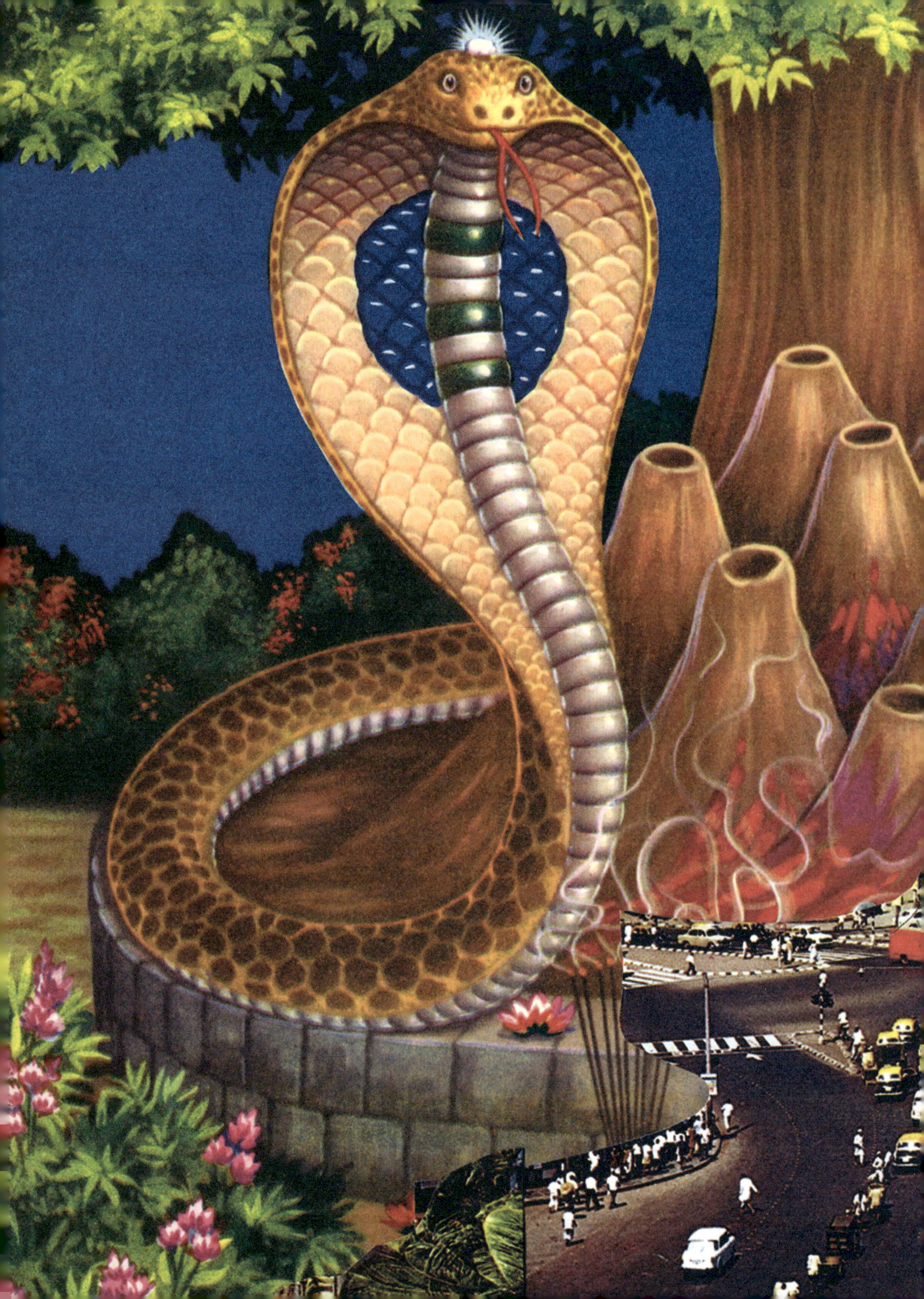